REMEMBERING

Len Berg's

Restaurant

A Second Helping

REMEMBERING

Len Berg's

Restaurant

A SECOND HELPING

Marie J. Amerson

Sandspurhill
Macon, Georgia 2019

Marie J. Amerson
PO Box 26364
Macon, Georgia 31221

Revised Edition

Remembering Len Berg's Restaurant: A Second Helping
Revised Edition With Additional Recipes

ISBN: 978-09894116-5-3

Revised edition published by the author 2019
First edition published by Mercer University Press 2012

Contents

PARTICULAR
PEOPLE DINE

at

Len Berg's

in the

POST OFFICE ALLEY
MACON, GA.

ACKNOWLEDGEMENTS

I became part of the Len Berg's Restaurant family more than forty years ago. I am honored to have an opportunity to put words on the page to record the history of a place so dear to me. Some words came from my mother-in-law, Celia Amerson, and restaurant family members Buster Barry, Annie Mae Mitcham, and Glenda Elliott. Descendants of Leonard Berg—Mary Anne Berg Richardson, Leonard Lee Berg, and Susan Berg Frenzel—kindly shared memories of the man who started it all, and employees at the Washington Memorial Library helped search for written information about the history of Macon. My parents, Ida and Harley Jones, did not share knowledge of Len Berg's Restaurant, but long ago they gave me a love of reading and a passion for recording family history. I appreciate all of these people for adding ingredients to the stew.

Being successful at putting words together to make sense is best achieved with the help of friends who are willing to read early drafts and make suggestions. Thank you Sandy Flatau, Sandy Gilreath, Lissie McAninch, Mary Nelle McLennan, and Mary Ann Siller for your encouragement and support.

Mercer University Press graciously accepted the manuscript for the first edition of this book. Their editors and design team created a beautiful book, and I am forever grateful to them all.

Pictures are truly worth a thousand words. The Berg, Barry, and Amerson families; Ken Hill; and the Middle Georgia Archives at Washington Memorial Library in Macon, Georgia, helped season this effort with images of people important to the Len Berg's story.

There would be nothing to say and no need for words at all if not for the employees who kept Len Berg's going for almost a century, as well as the "particular people" who dined at the restaurant through the years. A heartfelt thank you to all who made the business a success!

Most of all, my loving husband, Jerry, has been the heart and soul behind my effort to preserve the history of Len Berg's. Thank you for your patience as I put these words on the page, thank you for helping me select photos and remember stories, and thank you for all those wonderful meals through the years.

Each June, a billboard greeted visitors to Macon. Many knew they would find the Home Made Fresh Peach Ice Cream at Len Berg's Restaurant in the Post Office Alley. (c. 1982)

In 2010 I began writing the story of a special place, Len Berg's Restaurant in Macon, Georgia. I knew there were plenty of people who thought the restaurant was special, and it was an honor to work with Mercer University Press to publish *Remembering Len Berg's Restaurant* in 2012. The first edition sold out and the publisher offered the book in "print-on-demand" format for a while. When the publisher returned the book rights to me in 2019, I decided to find a way to serve up a "second helping" of Len Berg's stories.

One reason to publish this second edition about Len Berg's Restaurant is the opportunity to add a few more stories, tales that I did not hear until after the first edition was published. My hope is that this edition will generate special memories for readers who can say, "Oh, but she didn't tell the story about …" If readers share their own special memories with friends and family, then I will feel that they left the table with a full stomach *and* a full heart. It will be much like the sign of a successful restaurant described by my father-in-law, Jeff Amerson: customers had enough food to satisfy their hunger and their meal was so good that they wanted to return for more.

At the end of Chapter Six in the original edition of *Remembering Len Berg's Restaurant*, I wrote, "As they hold Len Berg's as a place in memory, many people will think of the building, the people, the celebrations, and more, but they will hold closest their memories of Len Berg's food."

People still ask about favorite menu items. Recipes for many of those appeared in the original book, but I failed to include several of the most popular. Also, as part of the publication process, two recipes appeared with an incorrect list of ingredients. This edition includes all of the recipes from the first book, including corrected recipes for Barbecued Short Ribs of Beef (page 101) and the Len Berg's Epic Salad Dressing (page 64). Recipes added to this edition appear in Chapter Six. I hope you find your favorite Len Berg's recipes, and if not, contact me so I can search to see if they are available.

Please note that I offer Len Berg's recipes as completely and correctly as possible based on notes made by the kitchen staff of a restaurant that served hundreds of meals each day. Those cooks rarely looked at a recipe, but rather, they prepared food by memory with a lot of heart and soul. In some cases, I converted amounts to reflect the needs of a kitchen feeding a family rather than a restaurant, but please understand, my only job at Len Berg's was doing taste tests! I have not attempted all of the recipes offered here, but many cooks find that a general list of ingredients will suffice for them to replicate a favorite dish. If you are such a cook, gather your favorite people around and enjoy a second helping from Len Berg's Restaurant!

Remembering Len Berg's Restaurant

INTRODUCTION TO FIRST EDITION

"H.M.F.P.I.C.—You Know Where." The sign appeared on June 1 as a signal it was time to head to Len Berg's Restaurant for a frozen blend of fresh local peaches and sweet cream. It would be on the menu for only a month, two at the most. The cryptic message on a billboard or in the local newspaper was part of the Macon, Georgia landscape for more than forty years. The restaurant that served the Home Made Fresh Peach Ice Cream, and a host of other Southern specialties, was a fixture in Macon for much longer—almost 100 years.

Jerry Amerson sold the business in 2003, and even today, he encounters people who remember his connection to Len Berg's Restaurant. Acquaintances ask what he has been doing since the sale and reminisce about the Filet Mignon, Lemon Meringue Pie, or Turkey and Dressing. A shoe salesman or bank employee trying to place his familiar face asks, "Didn't you work at Len Berg's?" Long Sunday afternoons prompt snowbirds to search him out by phone to say, "Every year when we drove from Indiana to Florida, we always stopped at Len Berg's for lunch."

And, on warm, almost summer days, just as the first Georgia peaches are reaching juicy perfection, former customers call to say they are thinking about Len Berg's. They want to tell Jerry stories about the restaurant or ask if he still has the recipe for Macaroon Pie or Epic Dressing or fresh peach ice cream.

People miss dining at the little brick building tucked back in an alley, and not just during ice cream season. They miss the food, the celebrations, and the friendly staff, folks who made them feel like a member of the family.

When he retired in 2003, Jerry Amerson had been the owner/operator of Len Berg's for ten years, and he had worked at the restaurant for more than twenty-five years. Before Jerry, his father, Jeff Amerson, was proprietor. The senior Amerson started working at Len Berg's in 1946 and purchased it from his mentor, Arthur P. Barry, in 1969.

Barry and his wife, Texas, bought the restaurant from the original owner in 1943 at a time when dining out was becoming more popular than ever in the United States. Their son, Buster, worked in the business several years as well.

If asked about the owners of Len Berg's Restaurant, most people would remember Jeff and Jerry Amerson or Art and Buster Barry. Only a few would remember the original owner, and many who didn't know him wondered about the restaurant's name. Was it a misspelled attempt to honor Charles Lindbergh? Was the name spelled as a single word or two? Even when they were told it was named after Leonard Berg, some people wanted to know if Berg was a shortened form of Bergman or Bergdorf or some other familiar name.

The original owner, Leonard Berg, operated public dining rooms, clubs, and saloons in Macon from as early as 1908. As he built his career, the establishments were identified by various names—the Saratoga, the Buffeteria, Len Berg's Chili Parlor—but wherever Berg offered food and drink, customers referred to it as "Len Berg's place."

What follows is a look at the dream Berg built in Macon, a restaurant that served the city for generations. It begins with a profile of the founder along with a glimpse into the history of his hometown. The history follows Berg's restaurant experiences in the early years of the twentieth century with Prohibition, the Great Depression, two World Wars, and more. Berg's legacy and the story continue through the ownership of two other families and ends with a hope that Len Berg's will hold a special place in the memory of the generations who enjoyed this iconic Southern restaurant.

Sketch by the author

Leonard Berg (c. 1910)

CHAPTER ONE

Leonard Berg

Restaurant founder Leonard Berg, or Len as he was known by most, was a native of Macon, Georgia. His father and uncle immigrated to the area from Bamburg, Germany, around 1867. Bernhardt Berg operated a wholesale tobacco business that required him to travel a great deal, and his brother Maro was listed in city records as a "capitalist." Both men became pioneers in the Macon Jewish community.

In 1873 Bernhardt married Julia Newton. Julia was a member of the Episcopal faith, so the couple had both a Rabbi and a Priest perform the wedding ceremony. Born in Fayette County, Georgia, and orphaned at an early age, Julia lived with a brother in Alabama for a time before moving to Macon to live with her sister, Elizabeth Avant. Her obituary in 1933 indicated she lived in Macon for sixty years.

Bernhardt and Julia had several children, but only four lived to be adults: Joe, Charles, Josephine, and their youngest son Leonard, who was born April 17, 1885.

In 1901 the Bergs settled in Cutter's Green, an area in East Macon that later became the site for the Coliseum (known in more recent years as the Centreplex). Len's father, Bernhardt, died at the age of fifty-four in 1903, the same year the youngest Berg left Macon and traveled west. Macon experienced a period of growth while Len was gone, and when he returned several years later, he and his mother lived on Spring Street for a few years.

Len and his brothers provided for Julia, and like many widows of her time, she supplemented the income with money she earned as a dressmaker. After his oldest brother, Joe, died of pneumonia in 1911, Len became the primary financial provider for his mother. She continued to reside in his home for the rest of her life, even after he married Willie Lee Darby in 1910. The young Bergs started raising a family of sons: Joe, born in 1915, Bernard, born in 1918, and James, born in 1923. The Berg family lived at various addresses in downtown Macon: Pine Street in 1911; Broad Street, 1914-1915; First Street, 1917; and Third Street, 1918-1922. In 1923, Berg purchased a lot on Nottingham Drive, drafted floor plans on the back of an old shoebox, and oversaw construction of the house where he lived until his death in 1948.

Len's brother Charles, who usually resided at his workplace, often visited the Bergs and shared a meal with the family. In the 1930s, he lived in his brother's Nottingham Drive home for a while. Their sister, Josephine, returned to Macon when her husband died unexpectedly, bringing her young daughter to live with Len and his family. Like her mother, Josephine used her skills as a seamstress and milliner to help with the family budget.

Like many young brides, Willie Lee Darby did not know how to cook when she married Berg in 1910. But, with a house full of family and her husband's coaching, Willie learned quickly. The Berg grandchildren remembered she was an excellent cook, and they especially enjoyed her chop suey, one of Len's signature dishes at the restaurant. During their thirty-eight years of marriage, Willie did a remarkable job managing the diverse household while Len focused on managing his business.

Len Berg put in long hours at the restaurant, working through both lunch and dinner shifts because he felt the public demanded real service. He kept a cot under the counter for the nights when he stayed on the premises to protect his business from unscrupulous workers or thieves who might see an empty building as an invitation to steal. Berg's sons grew up witnessing his strong work ethic and the passion that fueled his business success. They saw that he was a man who knew what it meant to be in charge, and they learned from him about drive and ambition. The Bergs sent their sons to college (not an easy thing to do during America's Great Depression), where Joe studied medicine, Bernard studied history, and James studied architecture.

Len Berg had registered for the draft in 1918, but he was not among the 4.8 million men called to serve during World War I. During the Second World War, though, he saw all three of his sons serve in the military.

As he raised his sons and supported extended family, Leonard Berg spent years learning the food-service trade, an industry that was evolving. The *Macon City Directory* often reported where Len Berg lived, but not always his occupation. Some years, the data indicated Berg was the manager of a particular establishment and other times left it to the restaurant or saloon to identify him as the proprietor. For a few years, Berg's name did not appear in the directory at all.

Len Berg owned property in Florida, so he might have been working there when the annual directory data was collected during the years when his name does not appear. There were a few occasions when the directory indicated Berg's occupation as "farmer," perhaps because of his truck farm near Bradenton, Florida. It might also have been because Berg purchased two milk cows and three calves in 1912 and kept a goat and chickens at their home on Nottingham Drive.

In addition to missing occasional entries in the local directory, Berg was absent from the 1910 and 1920 census reports for Georgia. Those periods might reflect time he spent learning the restaurant business in other locales. Berg's youngest son remembered traveling to Chicago once to visit his father, perhaps while Len was working there. But, regardless of where Berg traveled, he always returned home to Macon to operate a restaurant and raise a family.

The 1920s brought difficult times for many restaurant owners in the United States, and tough Prohibition years were followed by the Great Depression of the 1930s. Berg survived, and in 1932 he finally opened a restaurant under his own name. He commissioned a rising young architect to design a new building for his restaurant in 1936. Years later, architect Ellamae Ellis League recalled Berg as a great storyteller and a personable, congenial fellow. She spoke of his great vision for the future, and the final drawing they created in 1937 served the restaurant well for more than sixty years.

The architect was not alone in her positive impressions of Berg. Many friends knew him as a member of Mulberry Street Methodist Church and the Fraternal Order of Eagles. Some recalled how he spoke with a twinkle in his piercing blue eyes, and they knew him as a man who held strong convictions. While he did not hesitate to speak his mind, the restaurateur's actions also told a story. For instance, on May 4, 1937, the headline for a small front-page story in the local paper said, "Len Berg Hits Standing Auto, Reports Damage." The news account explained that Berg had damaged the fender of another automobile as he backed his car out of a parking space on Poplar Street. When he could not locate the owner of the car, Berg called the police station to report the incident. The article quoted Berg. "If he [the owner] makes a complaint, tell him I did it and will be glad to arrange settlement with him."

Berg expected the same integrity from his employees, and in exchange for meeting his high expectations, he paid a reasonable salary. Even during the depressed economic climate of the 1930s. Berg once noted with pride that although his restaurant was located off the main streets of Macon, not a single one of his employees lived in an alley.

By the end of the 1930s Berg had transitioned his business to a clientele that consisted of businessmen having lunch during the day and parties or couples dining out in the evening. He still spent a great deal of time at the restaurant, and the wear of more than thirty years in the food service business began to take its toll. In the early part of the 1940s, Berg saw Camp Wheeler put back into commission to train soldiers for another war, one in which his sons might be called to duty. He considered how to end his career in the restaurant business.

After more than thirty-five years of serving Macon diners, Berg sold his restaurant in 1943. He worked with the new owner for only a week before stepping away from his lifelong career, then he worked a few years as a wholesale liquor distributor with longtime friend, Whiskey Simmons.

Five years after Len Berg sold the restaurant bearing his name, he suffered a heart attack and died at his beloved home on Nottingham Drive on January 14, 1948. His name, though, lived on for years to come.

CHAPTER TWO

Len Berg's Restaurants: 1908-1932

Leonard Berg's name became synonymous with good Southern food, and his namesake became an icon in Macon, Georgia: Len Berg's Restaurant.

When Berg began building his dream in Macon in 1908—operating saloons, cafes, and restaurants in the area near Cherry and Mulberry Streets—he often worked for other men. He learned the purpose and structure of food service of the era, and just as landscapes and communities evolved over time, Berg and his business changed through the years to fit the needs of his community.

Macon, Georgia, was established in 1823, more than forty years before Berg's father immigrated to the area in 1867. When young Len was sixteen years old in 1901, his hometown began to experience growth surges, just like other parts of the country. According to *History of Macon, Georgia (1823-1949)*, written in 1950, "Many present day business institutions had their origin in the period between 1901 and 1907" (Young et al. page 445). Berg had moved to Texas around 1903, and much like the oil-boom in that state, the cotton industry brought rapid

growth to Macon. The decade beginning with 1906 saw a bustling downtown Macon, and the "Greater Macon" slogan of 1907 became a fitting call for Berg's return home.

The city was a transportation and commerce center in Georgia. The Ocmulgee Levee Company formed in 1906 to help maintain the river as a route for freight service, and Central Railroad shops formed in 1907 to meet the needs of the various railroads that passed through Macon. Several years later, the railroad companies constructed the centralized Terminal Station. Cotton farmers brought their loads through town along Cotton Avenue, and the brokers warehoused bales of cotton near the railroad terminal or on Wharf Street. (Wharf Street was later named Ocmulgee Street and then Riverside Drive.)

Macon saw a steady increase in the number of miles of paved city streets. Granite Belgian pavers or red brick pavers created bumpy, cobbled roads, but they vastly improved the muddy red clay streets of earlier days. In 1909, Macon was tagged as the center of the "Good Road Movement" in Georgia. Cherry

Street, with the railroad tracks and terminal at one end, became Macon's retail center, though it was not the only street with shops. F.W. Woolworth's Department Store on Cherry faced competition from the Empire Department Store on Third Street and Dannenberg's Department Store (built in 1906) on Cotton Avenue. Businesses advertising in a 1908 issue of the *Macon Daily Telegraph* included Joseph N. Neel Clothiers, Coleman Buggy Company, Equitable Banking and Loan, Schofield Iron Works, American National Bank, The Macon Shoe Company, and grocer W.L. Henry.

Construction began on the marble Federal Building on Mulberry Street in 1906, and postal operations started in the building in 1908. The Dempsey Hotel on Cherry Street was built in 1912, and the all-important Terminal Station was constructed in 1916. Wholesale grocers located their stores near the railroad and the downtown hotels on Poplar and Fourth Streets, positioning them close to the cafes and boarding houses nearby. Walnut Street was a residential area and home to many early Macon families while Mulberry Street featured Macon's first public library, the Grand Opera House, and several churches.

It was this period—between 1900, when Macon's population was more than 23,000, and 1910, when it grew to almost 41,000—

that Len Berg began his food-service career. The next decade brought even more growth as Macon annexed outlying communities: East Macon, West Macon, Napier Heights, Vineville, and more. New people came to Macon seeking employment in the cotton industry or construction jobs in the booming city. As they settled in, many of these new residents found Len Berg's place in a downtown alley, and because this was an era when food service focused on the needs of weary travelers, Berg offered food and drink to many Macon visitors as well.

Travelers came to Macon for business, but some also sought entertainment. Because the city hosted the important cotton industry, roads and railroads led into Macon from every direction, making it the ideal site for the annual Georgia State Fair.

The State Fair offered entertainment in the form of band concerts, a balloon ascension, and races, and many families scheduled their visit to coincide with the opening of "Happy Street" at Central City Park. Though it was much smaller in scale than the 1904 World's Fair at St. Louis, Missouri, or the 1901 Pan American Exposition in Buffalo, New York, the Georgia State Fair offered fairgoers a glimpse of exciting new products and industries. For instance, at the 1908 State Fair, visitors who arrived in mule-drawn wagons or by horse and buggy could order a

"White Steamer" automobile from agent John S. Schofield.

People who traveled a "fur piece" to visit Macon, whether for the fair or for business, probably spent at least one night in the city. If they did not have friends or family to put them up, visitors stayed at one of the hotels or boarding houses downtown. Historically, such accommodations provided food to guests in their lunchrooms. Inns and taverns provided food for travelers. Saloons or taverns catered food service to their customers who came for drinks, and usually, the establishment did not charge for the food. (Most often, saloon and tavern customers were men, since it would have been improper for an unescorted woman to visit such a place.) A pot of chili or servings of hot tamales would have been hearty food choices and spicy enough to encourage a man to order another drink. It was good business.

In the early part of the twentieth century, locals rarely ate in public dining rooms. Stand-alone restaurants, with individual tables and service, were rare. In Macon, the 1907 City Directory catalogued far more saloons and lunchrooms than restaurants—seven restaurants, thirty-three lunchrooms, and sixty-nine saloons. This continued to be the trend during the first two decades of the 1900s.

One establishment included in the 1907 data was the Berg and Hancock Saloon at 602 Fourth Street. Len's brother Charles partnered with a man named John Hancock to operate the business. Charles might have coaxed his younger brother back home to work at the saloon because Len worked there for a brief period in 1908 before moving on to other establishments, including Macon's Teutonia Club. After several years, Len managed a saloon owned by Thomas Brooks.

Berg's earliest years in Macon's food-service culture came at a time when America was trying to determine how it felt about the sale of alcohol. Whiskey and liquor dealers advertised heavily in the daily newspaper, their ads appearing on the same pages as one-cent-per-word classifieds where men might be looking for work. A sampling from the October 29, 1908, *Macon Daily Telegraph* advertised Sam and Ed Weichselbaum's whiskeys and brandies, and The Altmayer and Flatau Liquor Company, which highlighted their Old Georgia Corn. Clarke's Pure Rye from Clarke Brothers & Company was promoted as "aged and bottled by the Government," and "Sunny Brook Whiskey—The Pure Food" was suggested for medicinal use. The same page carried an ad for Dr. Woodley's Sanitorium, where whiskey and opium addiction were treated without shock. The temperance movement was adamant about the destructive nature of alcoholic beverages, but the food business had not yet decided the appropriate course of action—alcohol sales were good for business.

Food service in the early 1900s focused first on beverages, then on food, and Berg offered familiar foods to his customers—sandwiches and soups. In addition to the standard fare, though, Berg enjoyed putting exotic dishes on the menu for adventurous eaters, dishes like authentic Texas Chili or Chop Suey.

The period of the early 1900s also provided a change in the way Americans thought about dining out in general. Cafes and dining rooms shifted from being frequented mainly by travelers to becoming a setting in which friends could socialize. The 1904 World's Fair (the St. Louis Exposition) featured a wonderful array of such eateries and highlighted foods like ice cream cones, hamburgers, Dr. Pepper, iced tea, peanut butter, and Texas-style chili. Such foods certainly existed before 1904, but they became more popular as a result of the fair. So did dining out.

Electricity and the introduction of electric refrigeration, which helped serve the dining needs of the masses who attended the 1904 World's Fair, became more widely available throughout the country. Like cities all across America, Macon saw an increase in lunch rooms and cafes, where businessmen could find a noon-day meal, but it would be a few more years before restaurants with a more formal sense of guest service became a common part of the landscape. In Macon in 1908 Loh's Cafe at 516 Mulberry Street boasted in an advertisement that it was the "only first-class restaurant in the city for Ladies and Gentlemen."

Just as the restaurant industry changed, Len Berg evolved in the food-service business. He worked first as a candy-maker for Johnson K. & Company, a confectioner who advertised in a 1904 *Macon Telegraph*, "We ask the trade to bear in mind that we are headquarters for all kinds of candies. Our big factory is fully equipped and running every day. Order of us and get fresh made goods. We sell only to dealers." Berg likely worked in the factory and then as a salesman. Later, he worked for Lowney's Candies, a company famous for specialty candies including the Chocolate Cherry Blossom.

It might have been his work as a distributor for Johnson-K & Company or Lowney's that took Berg west in 1903. In 1905 the young man found himself flat broke in Houston, Texas. He telegraphed a businessman, who had placed an ad in the local paper there, and cited his experience as a confectioner. The businessman wired Berg enough money to travel by train from Houston to

Beaumont, Texas. When he arrived in the oil-boom town of Beaumont, Berg found his new job was not in the usual candy-making factory. His new employer operated a newsstand, candy store, and eatery out of a large tent. Berg's work as a confectioner placed him alongside a Mexican woman preparing meals for the oil workers, and it was his co-worker who taught him recipes with a Tex-Mex kick.

After a few years in Beaumont, Berg returned to Macon and began serving Texas chili and hot tamales, recipes that "made the town sit up and take notice" ("Romancing in Business") for the next twenty-six years.

In 1911, the year after city leaders added street lights to Cherry Street, Berg found his way to Wall Street. He managed the Teutonia Club, located at 553 Wall Street, an alley between Mulberry Street and the "Great White Way" of Cherry (called thus because of its bright street lights.) The Teutonia Club was located on Wall Street from as early as 1907 through at least 1912, when it moved to Mulberry Street. Throughout many communities in the United States, Teutonia Clubs often served as social hubs for German immigrants. Members of Macon's Teutonia Club, dressed in suits and straw hats, would gather to play pinochle and drink beer.

One source suggested Berg started his career at the Saratoga, where he employed twenty-two workers. His association with the Saratoga at 36 Wall Street was cited in a 1913 civil court case. Berg was identified as proprietor of the Saratoga Buffet, a "blind tiger where spiritous malt and intoxicating liquors are sold in violation of the law." Five years later, the Saratoga Hotel and Restaurant was located at 552 ½ Mulberry Street, but W.B. Medlin was named as the proprietor. In 1920, still another proprietor was listed for The Saratoga, and as late as 1968, a restaurant with that name continued to operate on a corner of Wall Street.

The name "Saratoga" might have been selected for a Macon restaurant to conjure images of the famous New York political and social hub of the era. Berg might also have associated the name with his time in Beaumont, Texas, home of the Saratoga Oil & Pipe Line Company that advertised shares of capital stock in the Macon newspaper in 1901, a few years before he journeyed west.

By 1914 Berg was a clerk at Thomas Brooks' saloon at 550 Wall Street, and in 1918 the *Macon City Directory* noted he was employed at a cafe at 26 Wall Street. When Berg registered for the 1918 draft, he reported himself to be a self-employed lunch producer and the site of his business was 26 Wall Street. Berg's brother Charles registered for the draft the same year, noted the same location for employment (and residence), but he listed C.H. Smith as his employer. The directory indicated C.H. Smith was the proprietor of a cafe at 26 Wall Street, and Charles Berg continued to work with Smith through the reporting period for the 1920 publication of the city directory.

Whether he was the proprietor or clerk at Brooks' saloon, Leonard Berg was forging his way into the dining scene of Macon. A small faded card (reported to be circa 1908, but probably from a later date) boasted Berg as proprietor of a Wall Street eatery with a fifteen-cent lunch plate, beverages sold in cold steins, and "service unsurpassed. Everything new, neat and clean." Perhaps the ad posted news of the private Teutonia Club, or it may have been advertising the Buffeteria.

Some accounts suggest that Berg's first restaurant in Macon was called the Buffeteria. He was identified in the city directory as manager of the Buffeteria in 1924, and family members stated that in the early days, Berg operated a restaurant by that name. A 1934 unpublished article described Berg's business and called attention to the electric "Buffateria" sign on the corner of his building pointing the way for diners.

Berg's food service evolved, as it did in the rest of the country, from serving only weary travelers or men in taverns to catering to clientele who were interested in the social experience of dining out. As Prohibition gripped the country, saloons, taverns, and bars reconfigured themselves into cafes, soda shops, and tea rooms. Restaurants and clubs that had previously relied on alcohol sales shifted their attention to high-volume food sales.

In April 1923 the *Macon Telegraph* celebrated a rise in the number of eating places in the city: "Eating Houses About as Numerous Now as Bars in Former Days" headlined an article that said there were twenty-five eating houses in three blocks on Cherry Street from Cotton Avenue to the Terminal Station. The article noted new establishments "from the wiener stand to the severely fashionable hotel grill" and suggested that "during the rushing age of 1923, the number of feet under the old home table has been diminished by the lure of the bright restaurant lights."

The article also quoted one restaurant owner's so-called "sage" advice: "Don't divorce your wife because she can't cook; eat here and save her for a pet."

At the time of the 1923 article, Berg was managing the Buffeteria. His brother Charles lived and worked as a clerk in the restaurant.

The establishment might have been, as the article noted, a quiet home-like diner that brought "memories of the things that mother used to cook," but Berg also offered chili and tamales, items not likely on the table of most Georgia cooks.

For a while, Berg's eatery was located on the northwest corner of Wall and Second Street Lane, but then he moved to the southeast corner of Wall and Third Street Lane. The Buffeteria at 449 Wall Street was a half-block off the beaten path mentioned in the article, and it was one of sixty-seven restaurants listed that year in the *Macon City Directory*. Wall Street (which came to be known as Mulberry Street Lane), did not have prominent buildings like architect Neil Reid's skyscraper on Mulberry or the hotels and cotton brokers of Poplar Street, but it was home to a variety of other businesses, the kind that helped Macon function on a daily basis. Many of Berg's customers were working men from the nearby garage or blacksmith, machine shop or electric company.

Berg was not identified as the proprietor of either the Saratoga or the Buffeteria when they garnered attention from federal revenuers in 1927 and 1928. The Saratoga Buffet was padlocked in 1927, and the *Macon Telegraph* reported on raids at the Buffeteria, where officers located a cache of bottled liquor, a secret passage to an underground gopher, and a bell to ring as a warning when federal agents raided the place. Records indicate another man owned the Wall Street business, and though the *Macon City Directory* listed Berg as being in the food service business at the time, it did not name the establishment where he worked. The business at 449 Wall Street sat vacant for several years after the 1928 raid, until 1932 when loyal customers finally saw Berg's name over the door.

For almost twenty-five years Berg managed, clerked, or operated a variety of eateries in Macon. People came to expect good food at "Len Berg's Place," no matter who owned the business, and they were accustomed to finding his place in an alley. In 1932 they were not disappointed to find the establishment at 449 Wall Street formally identified as Len Berg's.

Leonard Berg (c. 1943)

A Second Helping

CHAPTER THREE

Len Berg's Restaurant: 1932-1943

In 1932 Len Berg's Chili Parlor opened at a location familiar to loyal customers. Two years later, the chili parlor located at the southeast corner of Wall Street and Third Street Lane changed its name to Len Berg's Cafe.

Berg began his food-service career at a time when men made up the bulk of the work force in the city and most customers were male. Public dining rooms and taverns or saloons catered to men, and it was unusual for women to dine in such establishments. When Prohibition brought changes to the restaurant industry, though, it became more acceptable for women to dine in the cafeterias, luncheonettes, or tea rooms that cropped up. More women were joining the general work force, too, and in 1927 the journal *Restaurant Management* reported that cafes and restaurants employed more women as servers as their female patronage reached close to sixty percent.

Berg expanded his menu to satisfy the diverse customer base that now included more women. In 1934 an unpublished article addressed to "the News, Macon, GA" referred to Berg's business as a "Buffateria" (sic) where he served "palate tickling dishes for the epicure" and described the eatery:

> During the evening when you see those fine motors turning up the alley beside the Union, or on Third Street beside Burden Smith's, or on Mulberry beside Rogers, or on Broadway beside the Douglas [sic] theatre; they are going to Len Berg's—for something different in the food line—the popular standbys, chili and hot tamales, or the Chinese dish, chop suey, or any of the other dishes for which Len is famed.
>
> At noon time, men who are cranky about their food and must eat downtown, go over to Len's for his 30¢ plate lunch. … When they are alone, the men eat in the first floor lunch room. When they bring their wives at night, they go upstairs to the private dining rooms. Much of the evening trade comes in parties of two, three, or four couples.

This write-up appeared in a typed 1934 article, possibly prepared for a reporter at the *Macon News*. It was titled "Romancing in

Business" and the document, which was found in family papers, referred to Berg's twenty-six years operating a restaurant in Macon after his return to the city in 1908. It catalogued Berg's varied menu, which represented familiar foods alongside more unique dishes with an international flair: plain chop suey was thirty-five cents; Mussolini spaghetti, Italian spaghetti Caruso style, and Italian ravioli, fifty cents; hot tamales, fifteen cents; chili, fifteen to twenty cents; Mexican soup, ten cents; "midget" tenderloin steak with potato cake, ten cents; corn beef and cabbage, forty cents; and Irish stew, fifteen cents.

The menu also would have included coffee, sweet iced tea, or sweet soft drinks, and Berg was known to be a stickler about the beverages he served. He did not want his coffee to sit for long periods in a large urn, so he used two-quart percolators to brew it. His method might also have been a tactic to prevent waste, since in the period of the 1930s, Americans could not afford to waste anything, especially a good cup of coffee.

The financial crisis of America's Great Depression was not a period of starvation, but it was a time of cutting back. Restaurants in the South might have fared better than other regions of the country because they had a greater supply of fresh vegetables, but eating out was a luxury many citizens could

not afford. Still, businessmen and those who held onto a job had to eat. Berg adjusted his menu to fit the available supplies and posted specials on a daily menu board. He managed through the worst of the economic slump, and by the spring of 1936 Berg was ready to realize the next phase of his career.

Berg commissioned a local architect to formalize the design of a new building for his restaurant. Though Ellamae Ellis League rejected an emphasis on her gender, she was a pioneer of architecture in the South. A single parent, she apprenticed with a local firm from 1922-1927 and then traveled to France to study. When she returned from the Ecole des Beaux-Arts in Fontainebleu, League continued to apprentice for a period, earned her professional registration as an architect in 1934, and opened her own practice. League's early designs included a service station, residences in Macon and surrounding areas, churches, schools, and a new restaurant for her friend Leonard Berg.

Many years later, when Berg's granddaughter interviewed the architect for a history project, League talked about the restaurateur's vision and creativity. Berg, who had drawn plans for the home he and his wife built on Nottingham Drive, had definite ideas for the restaurant's design. Reflecting League's philosophy, which incorporated function and aesthetics, the architectural design utilized Berg's experience and ideas as well as her own flair with French provincial elements to ensure a pleasing form.

Berg and League designed the new restaurant with a lunch counter near the kitchen and up to eight private dining rooms. Two of the private rooms were large enough to be divided with a folding door to create two additional dining rooms. The 1936 drawing had the footprint for a long, narrow lot, but when Berg leased property from sisters May and Martina Burke in 1937, the site on the corner across from 449 Wall Street did not stretch the full length of the alley to Cherry Street. League completed a second set of drawings on May 25, 1937, depicting Len Berg's Cafe at "Wall Street at Union Alley." (The reference to Union Alley reflected the common name given to Third Street Lane because of its location next to the Union Department Store that faced Cherry Street.)

League's new design for the restaurant at 452 Wall Street depicted a building that would be sixty by one-hundred feet. The restaurant featured a central lunch counter with seating for ten, but it now had a hall on each side of the central portion that led to six dining rooms, three on each side. Each room had tables or booths to seat sixteen to twenty people, and a pair of swinging doors closed off the small rooms to allow customers to dine in private. The design called for wiring a radio loudspeaker in each room and a bell by the door so patrons could call for service.

Berg contracted with W.A. Stillwell, Jr., and League oversaw construction of the new restaurant in 1937. (While a newspaper article in 1950 cited 1935 as the year this construction took place, League's design wasn't completed until March 1937, and the property lease was signed that year.) Much like Loh's Cafe in the early part of the century and the Oriole Dining Rooms that served Macon in 1923, the new Len Berg's Restaurant was about more than just serving food; it provided a pleasant social experience for diners who were, once again, willing to spend money on entertainment and dining out.

The Great Depression was over and Maconites were as eager as other Americans to celebrate. The 1930s had ushered in a fledgling movie industry, and Macon had several theaters to provide entertainment. Lucas & Jenkins Theatre Company operated several venues in Macon, including the Capitol, the city's first modern theater, which seated 950 guests. The company collaborated with Len Berg's Cafe to advertise and encourage couples to entertain themselves with dinner and a movie. A small card billing shows at The Capitol in 1939 promoted Shirley Temple in *Susannah of the Mounties* or Lawrence Olivier and David Niven in *Wuthering Heights* at a cost of twenty-five cents for each ticket. The billing also advertised steaks and chops offered for dinner at Len Berg's Cafe and suggested a three-course lunch for thirty-five cents.

Berg did not post ads in the local newspapers, but he used other forms of advertising to ensure his restaurant continued to attract new customers as well as his loyal patrons. Arthur Lewis noted, in a history of his friend's restaurant, "With the increased facilities for serving the public, the fame of the dishes served by Mr. Berg began to assert itself. Day after day and night after night, people of Macon and visitors in the city stood in line waiting for Len Berg's famous Chili, his Spaghetti a la Italiene, Chop Suey, Chow Mein, and most of all—the delicious steaks which he always personally cut" (Lewis, 1950).

Berg used a 1941 Lanier High School football program to attract attention to Len Berg's Cafe. The ad proclaimed: "Best Known Throughout the South, Len Berg's is a good place to eat." It directed customers to Wall Street at the rear of Burden-Smith Company and noted Berg's "Famous Mexican Chili, Hot Tamales, Italian Spaghetti, Chop Suey, Sea Food, and a Regular Menu of American Foods." If that was not enough to entice

customers, the ad included a quote from the owner: "I Eat My Own Food."

Though he might have attended the football games or movies where he advertised, Berg worked through both shifts with his employees and was on hand supervising whenever the restaurant was open. According to the Lewis history, "On those few occasions when he was ill and unable to be on duty, the restaurant was closed."

Berg encouraged his sons to pursue their dreams, and after 1941 all of them were doing so, with a side trip into the military. All three boys served during World War II, but none were stationed at Camp Wheeler, the installation just outside the Macon city limits. The camp had been de-commissioned after World War I, but it became an infantry replacement center in the early 1940s. Camp Wheeler also functioned as a prisoner of war camp. Soldiers and personnel associated with the military increased central Georgia's population as housing near the camp filled with families, and homeowners opened their houses to boarders. As young men went off to war, young women moved in to take over manufacturing jobs in the area, including work at the Naval Ordinance Plant.

Social activities for the young men and women were often restricted by military protocol, but the USO hosted dances and performances for soldiers at Camp Wheeler. (On a personal note, in the 1940s my mother performed several times with Uncle Ned and the Hayloft Jamboree. She entertained troops with her "poor folks's Minnie Pearl" skit.) The dances, movies, and window shopping downtown were new to rural youth accustomed to peanut boilings and cane grindings. So was dining out.

Military leadership directly impacted the choices for dining out as restaurants in the area came under new scrutiny for their sanitary conditions. In October 1942 the *Macon Telegraph* reported on a sweeping investigation of Macon eating establishments. The Army and board of health officials declared the sanitary conditions in restaurants, cafes, and drug stores in the area to be "very bad." The worst offenders were cited for violations and many were restricted from serving food to soldiers.

Len Berg's was among the approved locations where officials posted a placard noting its status as a "clean and sanitary establishment." Like the few other eateries approved by health officials, it experienced "the heaviest rush in history" as thousands of soldiers and civilians sought places to eat in Macon.

An official military stamp of approval was important, but Berg already operated his business in a manner Duncan Hines would have found satisfactory. Hines, often called America's first food critic, was a traveling salesman who was not impressed by fancy trappings or menus. He published an annual list of restaurants that met his approval, and just like the military and board of health, Hines focused on good food, reasonable prices, and sanitary dining facilities.

During the war, like other restaurateurs of the period, Berg faced a shortage of food because manufacturers first had to supply the needs of the military. He stretched the available food to serve the larger numbers of customers that resulted from his status as a militarily approved establishment, and Berg added a patriotic slogan to the bottom of his menus: "OK a Bond to KO a Jap." (Note that while this expression would be considered inappropriate today, this reflects accepted language of the era.)

The war-time menu reminded diners that Len Berg's served lunch between 12:00 and 2:30 PM, and for sixty-five cents, they could purchase "Fried Shrimp Shanghai A La Berg, Chef's Special Chicken Pan Pie, Baked Ham with Raisin Sauce, American Cheese Omelet, and Spaghetti with Italian Tomato Sauce." The luncheon price included two vegetables (baked potatoes, oven baked beans, turnip greens, or fruit salad), and iced or hot tea or coffee to drink. For an extra five cents, diners could have Coca-Cola or milk, although the menu noted "We regret the necessity of limiting patrons to one serving of one beverage." Desserts of the day were chocolate-topped ice cream or fresh peach cobbler.

The rush of patrons required Berg to move customers through quickly and efficiently so arriving customers did not have to wait an undue amount of time for a table. One written account suggested Berg often tiptoed from door to door to peep in where customers were inclined to sit and talk after they finished their meal. It suggested Berg hoped his appearance would encourage the group to move on. In later years, though, customers remembered a different version. Dawdling customers agreed that Berg peeped into the rooms to check on tables, and they recalled he would stop at a table with lingering guests. While Berg chatted with the group, though, he constantly bumped his knee against the table or their chair. Anxious to get away from such an annoying movement of the table, most diners cut the conversation short and bid farewell to Berg. If they stopped to speak to someone in the hall, the parting guests noted how Berg quickly called a new party to the cleared table.

Berg did not alter his practice of seating customers as they arrived, even when it involved military leaders or city matriarchs.

Once, when Berg seated a group of young soldiers before an Army captain and his party, he had to explain the restaurant's policy was "first come, first served." The offended officer suggested Berg had no respect for the military, to which Berg noted, "Rank means nothing to me—they were here first." The restaurateur did not bother to explain that all three of his sons were in the military (a captain, a sergeant, and a private).

On another occasion, Berg faced the wrath of a Macon socialite who wanted him to hold seating for visiting military dignitaries. She could not sway him by explaining, "But, General Hester will be one of the guests!" Berg noted he had a business to run, not a social club.

And after so many years of running such a demanding business, Berg knew well how to operate a successful restaurant. He knew how to keep people moving through, how to stretch available rations, and how to work with local officials to ensure he operated within their guidelines. Even as war took young men out of the general workforce, he knew how to find and keep employees to serve the increased numbers of diners. Berg knew all of that, but he also knew his sons would not be taking over the business when he decided to retire. They had seen the toll of such a demanding business, and all three pursued other careers.

After thirty-five years of serving the dining public, Len Berg and his business were well-established entities in Macon. No one in the community—including Berg—wanted to see his restaurant close. He would have to find someone outside his family to take it on, and in 1943 the man who spiced up Macon with his own brand of good food found that someone else.

Sign posted in Len Berg's Restaurant (c. 1940)

The Food

Len Berg's food can often be described by a word with Japanese origins: *umami*. The literal meaning of *umami* is "deliciousness" or "good flavor," and it refers to the fifth sense of taste, along with sweet, sour, salty, and bitter. The iconic Southern restaurant established by the son of a German Jewish immigrant was known for delicious food, and whether it was eight years or eighteen since you last ate at Len Berg's, you probably recall the *umami* taste of your favorite dish from the Macon, Georgia restaurant.

This is not a cookbook, but the story of Len Berg's would be incomplete without at least a sampling of recipes based on dishes prepared at the historic restaurant. In her book *Under the Tuscan Sun*, Frances Mayes shared instructions on various dishes she prepared in her summer home in Italy. She notes, "Much of what we do is too simple to be called a recipe—it's just the way we do it." If asked for a recipe for corn sticks or chili, stuffed shrimp or fried chicken, the Len Berg's staff might respond the same way.

The great Southern cooks of Len Berg's would probably describe their technique something like this:"We put ingredients together and cook for as long as needed." They might have seen recipes written for the dishes they prepared, but for the most part, the cooks learned from each other how Len Berg's seasoned the potato salad or black-eyed peas. They prepared so many salmon croquettes they knew how the mixture should feel before they dropped the patties into a hot pan. Annette knew better than to open the oven to check the rolls—she waited for the aroma to tell her it was time to take them out.

Len Berg's cooks cared about the food they sent out of the kitchen, and their results reflected Chef Wilbur Mitcham's philosophy about cooking: You had to show a lot of love.

The recipes that follow are relayed much as the cooks at Len Berg's would have taught them to a new employee. Sometimes, precise measurements are offered, but often, only general directions are provided. Experienced cooks will know how to adapt; novice cooks may want to refer to basic cooking instructions to better understand how to prepare some dishes. A few of the recipes make a large amount—enough to serve a restaurant crowd—but most have been cut down to a size appropriate to the family cook. Use reference materials to determine alternate measurements for smaller or larger quantities.

Enjoy, experiment, install a bell and post a sign in your kitchen that says "Press button to praise the cook." And remember the key ingredient in recipes from Len Berg's: a lot of love.

A Second Helping

RECIPES FROM THE BERG ERA

Chili

Hot Tamales

Italian Spaghetti
(Mussolini or Caruso Style)

Chop Suey

Shrimp a la Berg

Brownies

Rooftop neon atop Len Berg's Restaurant in the Post Office Alley, Macon, Georgia.

Chili

Leonard Berg took pride in serving unique dishes. When he returned to Macon in 1908, he offered real Texas chili, a recipe he learned from a Mexican woman who worked beside him in Beaumont, Texas. That original recipe is long gone, perhaps buried in the cornerstone of the 1950 building in the Post Office Alley. Chef Wilbur Mitcham, who started work at Len Berg's in 1947, shared the following Chili recipe. He adapted it to include contemporary ingredients and noted this was the version he served to the public. When Chef made chili for his own family, he preferred to add more heat. Berg also ladled his Texas chili on top of a filet mignon for a favorite menu item, "Steak-in-the-Red."

DIRECTIONS

Chop 3 stalks of celery, 3 green onions, 1 large bell pepper, 1 medium Spanish or Vidalia onion, and 1 tablespoon of garlic; add to a stock pot with about a tablespoon of oil and cook until soft. Add about 2 pounds of ground chuck and brown. Drain excess grease from the pot before adding the rest of the ingredients.

Add one 15-ounce can of tomato sauce, one 15-ounce can of chunky tomatoes (chili style), two 10-ounce cans of Rotel diced tomatoes with chili, one 6-ounce can of tomato paste, and one 16-ounce can of chili beans. Stir well and add 3 tablespoons chili powder, stirring again. Cover and simmer until the aroma tells you it's time to eat! Serve Len Berg's corn sticks on the side or crumbled into the hearty stew, or ladle chili over a steak.

As Chef suggested, add more chili powder if you prefer a spicier stew. However, because the tomatoes with chili come in various ranges of heat, taste to determine whether you really need the extra spice.

CHILI

INGREDIENTS

3 stalks celery

3 green onions

1 bell pepper

1 medium Spanish or Vidalia onion

1 Tbsp. garlic

1 Tbsp. oil

2 lbs. ground chuck

15 oz. can of tomato sauce

15 oz. can of chunky tomatoes

2 - 10 oz. cans of Rotel diced tomatoes with chili

6 oz. can of tomato paste

16 oz. can of chili beans

3 Tbsp. chili powder

Hot Tamales

HOT TAMALES

INGREDIENTS

3 pork roasts (4 lbs. each)

~~~~

Red Chili Filling:

1 ½ lbs. red chili pods

1 lb. lard or shortening

3 C. flour

10 Tbsp. ground cumin

salt and pepper, to taste

~~~~

Masa:

3-4 lbs. lard or shortening

20 lbs. corn meal

salt, to taste

9 Tbsp. baking powder

~~~~

cornhusks

Berg's Mexican co-worker in Texas also taught him how to make tamales, and the restaurateur included the unique offering at his Macon eatery, where it quickly became a signature dish. He even referred to himself as the Hot Tamale King of Macon!

The spicy meat wrapped in a cornmeal mixture (masa) and steamed in a corn-husk wrap was popular as a "carryout" food for working men in the South. The traditional Southwestern food traveled East in the early 1900s, and today, a website (www.tamaletrail.com) is dedicated to the Mississippi Delta Tamale Trail. The site includes a step-by-step hot tamale "how-to" with photos.

Tamales are labor-intensive for the average home kitchen. Women in the Southwest often gather to help one another through the process, much like gathering for a traditional quilting bee. They prepare the meat, the masa, the cornhusks. They wrap, and they cook, or prepare for the freezer, dozens of Tamales to serve or share as gifts at Christmas.

My friend Alicia McAninch from New Mexico always ran and hid when her mother said it was time to make tamales, so she shared this family recipe from her cousin Bea Valle. The traditional recipe is much the same as what Berg learned a hundred years ago in Texas, and it makes about 30-dozen tamales.

DIRECTIONS

Cook three pork roasts (average 4 pounds each) in a large roaster; set aside to cool.

While the pork is cooling, prepare a red-chile filling with 1 ½ pounds of red-chile pods. Cut the stem off each chile pod and clean out some of the seeds; wash the pods and put them in a large pan to boil until soft. Blend a few cooked pods at a time in a blender and run the mixture through a sieve to catch the remaining seeds and chile skins. In a large roasting pan, melt 1 pound of lard or shortening over low heat. Add 3 cups of flour for thickening; add chile, 10 tablespoons ground cumin, and salt and pepper to taste. Simmer 15 minutes.

When the pork is cooled, shred it and add to the chile mixture to simmer another 15 minutes. Remove from heat and allow the mixture to cool completely. It will be easier to add to the masa if you let it stand for about three hours. Also, it can be stored up to three days in the refrigerator or up to two months in the freezer.

To prepare the masa, melt 3 to 4 pounds of lard or shortening in a large saucepan. Put 20 pounds of corn meal (may be fresh or prepared) in a very large roasting pan or dishpan; add salt to taste and 9 tablespoons of baking powder to the corn meal. Pour melted lard or shortening over the dry ingredients. When the mixture is well moistened, mix with both hands as much as possible so the masa is a spreadable consistency. Cover the prepared masa with cloth and let stand at least 20 minutes.

Remove silks and clean cornhusks well BEFORE putting them in water to soak. Rinse well in hot water—multiple times—and keep moist for the assembly process. (Some recipes for tamales call for small 3- x 6-inch rectangles of parchment paper instead of cornhusks.)

Spread about 1 tablespoon of masa on the square end of a prepared cornhusk, making a small square patch that is not too thick. Add 1 heaping teaspoon of chile meat mixture in the middle of the masa square. Close the tamale by lapping over two sides of husk, then fold over long end of husk. You can use a loaf pan lined with paper towels to stand the prepared tamales until you are ready to pack them in freezer bags or start cooking.

To cook the tamales, line the bottom of a large pan with cornhusks that were too small to use in spreading masa. Put a tin cup upside down in the center of the pan and stand tamales all around the cup. Arrange the tamales to fill the sides; do not stack on top. Put 3 cups boiling water around the sides, and be careful to not put water directly on top of the tamales. Cover with a wet cloth and cook over low heat at least one hour. Watch carefully, and add more water as needed.

Tamales may be frozen, raw or cooked. If cooked, let the tamales cool before putting into freezer bags. If tamales are frozen raw, there is no need to defrost before cooking, although it may be necessary to separate them so they can be arranged in the pan for cooking.

Hot Tamales can be served "wet" (covered with chili) or "dry." They can be fried, and in a St. Louis diner, the waitress explained that some customers want their dry tamale to be served "greasy," with extra oil to add more flavor.

Be sure to use caution when you steam the tamales. Alicia McAninch recalled that when her mother and aunt prepared a batch in the 1950s, they used a homemade pan her father crafted from a flour canister. She heard a loud explosion from the kitchen just before the two women came running out covered in masa and chili sauce. No one was injured, but it took the rest of the day to clean up the kitchen. (Maybe that's why Alicia went running when it was time to make the tamales!)

Italian Spaghetti - Variations

Mussolini or Caruson Style

A 1934 article about the restaurant highlighted several items from Len Berg's menu that showed his interest in dishes with an international flavor. Entrees priced at fifty cents included "Italian Spaghetti Caruso Style," "Italian Ravioli," and "Mussolini Spaghetti." Long before Mussolini sided with Germany in World War II, he was credited with increasing the production of pasta in his homeland, and as the dish found its way to America, Mussolini Spaghetti became a popular recipe in the 1930s.

DIRECTIONS

Mussolini Spaghetti starts with a meat-and-tomato-sauce base, with fried eggplant cubes and chicken liver added. Stir the sauce into cooked spaghetti noodles and place the mixture in a flat oven-safe pan. Top with shredded mozzarella cheese and bake until the cheese is golden in color.

Caruso-Style Spaghetti features a traditional meat-and-tomato sauce. Add chopped chicken livers, sautéed mushrooms, Romano cheese, and sherry. Toss the sauce with the noodles, and sprinkle the plated spaghetti with cheese and basil before serving.

ITALIAN SPAGHETTI - VARIATIONS

INGREDIENTS

Mussolini Style:

meat and tomato sauce

fried eggplant cubes

chicken liver

cooked spaghetti noodles

Mozzarella cheese

~~~~

Caruson Style:

meat and tomato sauce

chopped chicken livers

sautéed mushrooms

Romano cheese

sherry

cooked spaghetti noodles

basil

Chop Suey

CHOP SUEY

INGREDIENTS

strips of meat (chicken, pork, or beef)

oil or fat

salt and pepper, to taste

3 stalks celery

1 or 2 large green peppers

1 or 2 large onions

2-3 Qts. chicken stock

12 C. of chop suey vegetables
(bean sprouts, water chestnuts, bamboo shoots, and mushrooms)

½ C. soy sauce

cornstarch

steamed rice

Len Berg's friend Reverend Burke was a missionary in China, and it might have been the reverend who inspired another of the restaurant's trademark dishes, chop suey. When Berg commissioned Ellamae Ellis League to draw plans for a new restaurant on Wall Street in 1937, she included a chop suey cooker between the cooking range and a hot grill on the back wall of the kitchen.

Chef Wilbur Mitcham often used the cooker—a large wok—to make chop suey from leftovers and serve Len Berg's staff. Wenzel's Menu Maker *explains that American versions of chop suey and chow mein are similar, with the distinction being that chow mein is generally served on or with fried noodles, and chop suey is served with rice.*

DIRECTIONS

In a large skillet or wok, brown ½- to 1-inch strips of meat (chicken, pork, or beef) in fat and season with salt and pepper. Slice 3 stalks of celery at a slant, chop 1 to 2 large green peppers and 1 to 2 large onions. Add to the meat to simmer about one minute. Add 2 to 3 quarts of chicken stock and bring to a boil. Drain a #10 can of chop suey vegetables (about 12 cups of bean sprouts, water chestnuts, bamboo shoots, and mushrooms) and add to the mixture. Mix in ½ cup of soy sauce as desired and a small amount of cornstarch to thicken the mixture.

Amounts can be adjusted for the vegetables and other ingredients you have on hand. Serve 8 ounces of chop suey with 4 ounces of steamed rice.

Shrimp a la Berg

A 1942 menu from Len Berg's Restaurant included "Fried Shrimp Shanghai a la Berg" as one of the featured entrees. Berg often tried new dishes for his customers, and "Shrimp Shanghai" and "Shrimp Newberg" were among the recipes once used at the establishment. Both recipes are offered here.

DIRECTIONS

Shrimp Newberg (spelled "Newburg" in traditional recipes) is a cream-based sauce served over boiled, de-veined shrimp.

For 1 to 2 pounds of fresh shrimp, assemble ingredients and prepare the following: In a medium saucepan, melt ¼ cup butter; blend in 2 ½ tablespoons of all-purpose flour or cornstarch to thicken. Season with ¾ teaspoon salt, a pinch of cayenne pepper, and a dash of nutmeg. Bring to a boil and cook, stirring, for about one minute. Gradually add 2 cups of half-and-half and 3 tablespoons of dry sherry; cook until thickened and smooth, stirring constantly. Stir about ⅓ cup of the hot mixture into 2 egg yolks that have been lightly beaten, then pour the tempered egg yolk mixture back into the saucepan with the remaining sauce. Add peeled and cooked shrimp to the mix and heat through, stirring constantly. Serve over toast or rice.

~~~~

Directions and ingredients for Shrimp Shanghai appear on the following page.

SHRIMP A LA BERG

INGREDIENTS

Shrimp Newberg:

1 to 2 lbs. peeled and deveined shrimp

¼ C. butter

2 ½ Tbsp. all-purpose flour or cornstarch

¾ tsp. salt

pinch cayenne pepper

dash nutmeg

2 C. half-and-half

3 Tbsp. dry sherry

2 egg yolks

toast or rice

Shrimp Shanghai:

1 to 2 lbs. peeled and deveined shrimp

3 eggs

1 Tbsp. Worcestershire sauce

1 C. soy sauce

juice of 1 lemon

1 Qt. milk

2 C. all-purpose flour

2 Tbsp. salt

½ Tbsp. black pepper

1 C. water

4 Tbsp. lemon juice

4 Tbsp. Wesson oil

½ C. beaten egg whites

frying oil

Shrimp Shanghai is a fried shrimp that has been marinated before breading.

Beat together 3 eggs, 1 tablespoon Worcestershire, 1 cup soy sauce, juice of 1 lemon, and 1 quart of milk. Place the peeled and de-veined shrimp in the marinade and leave for 30 minutes.

Remove shrimp from the marinade and roll dry before placing in the following batter.

Mix 2 cups all-purpose flour, 2 tablespoons salt, ½ tablespoon black pepper, 1 cup water, 4 tablespoons lemon juice, 4 Tablespoons Wesson oil. Mix well, and just before using, fold in ½ cup beaten egg whites. Dip shrimp in batter and fry.

Brownies

Lowney's Chocolates, founded in Boston by chocolate and cocoa purveyor Walter M. Lowney, popularized this moist, dense chocolate concoction at the 1901 Pan American Exposition in Buffalo, New York. As a young lad, Berg worked as a confectioner, and according to a 1930s article, he was the superintendent of "fancy-candy factories the length and breath (sic) of the land—for Lowney and other famous brands." ("Romancing in Business," 1934)

Though brownies did not appear on printed menus from Berg's period, he was a strong proponent of the dessert. He might have put his confectioner's experience to good use and tried this recipe from the 1907 Lowney's Cookbook *on his menu. After all, Berg often told his son James, "A meal without dessert is like a dance without music."*

BROWNIES

INGREDIENTS

2 oz. coarsely chopped unsweetened chocolate

½ C. unsalted butter

1 C. granulated sugar

½ C. all-purpose flour

¼ tsp. salt

2 large eggs

½ C. chopped pecans or walnuts (if desired)

DIRECTIONS

Preheat oven to 350 degrees and grease an 8-inch square baking pan. (You can also line the pan with non-stick foil or parchment.)

In a small, heavy saucepan, over lowest heat, melt 2 ounces coarsely chopped unsweetened chocolate; stir frequently until nearly melted. Immediately remove from heat and let cool slightly. (Check modern cookbooks for a method of melting the chocolate in a microwave.)

Use a large wooden spoon and work in a medium-sized bowl to beat together ½ cup unsalted butter, slightly softened, and 1 cup granulated sugar. Stir in the melted chocolate until it is smoothly incorporated. Stir in ½ cup all-purpose flour, ¼ teaspoon salt, and 2 large beaten eggs until well blended. Add ½ cup chopped pecans or walnuts, if desired. Pour the batter into a square baking pan and smooth the edges. Bake on the center oven rack for 19 to 23 minutes, until a toothpick inserted in the center comes out clean. Cool on a wire rack until thoroughly cooled. Cut into squares using a large sharp knife, wiping the knife clean between cuts.

This Brownie recipe makes sixteen 2x2-inch squares, which *Lowney's* suggested would keep for several days if packed airtight or up to a month if frozen.

The Barry Era: 1943-1969

Arthur P. Barry did not have a background in restaurant management when he and his wife purchased Len Berg's Cafe from the original owner in June 1943. He did, however, know his community and how to keep customers entertained and happy.

Art Barry was a native of New York City, where, in his youth, he tagged along with his nine brothers to swim in the city's East River. (They apparently left their one sister back at home during such adventures.) Later, Barry followed one of his brothers into the fledgling movie industry, a career that eventually landed him in Macon, Georgia.

Barry studied his brother's books to learn how to operate movie projectors and secured a job in the film industry in the 1930s. Lucas & Jenkins Theatres, which purchased Atlanta's Fox Theater in 1935 for its headquarters, distributed films for Hollywood and operated movie houses all over the Southeast. In Georgia, they had theaters from Elberton to Brunswick, Augusta to Atlanta, and Valdosta to Macon

where they bought the Ritz, Capitol, and Rialto theaters in 1931 and added The Grand in 1933. Barry worked for Lucas & Jenkins in North Carolina before moving to Lakeland, Florida, and then to Central Georgia. He became the Macon city manager for Lucas & Jenkins's four theaters, a job that required him to oversee operations of all the company's facilities in Macon. Before he left the firm in 1943, Barry had helped Lucas & Jenkins open a fifth movie house that was called The East Macon.

One aspect of the film industry gave Barry experience with food service. Not only was Lucas & Jenkins a leader in film distribution, but the firm, specifically, owner William Jenkins, was often credited with the idea of providing a full-service concession stand as part of the movie-going experience. Art Barry recalled in later years that popcorn sales often surpassed the profit from movie tickets in his theaters.

Popcorn sales and the concession stand gave Barry a taste of feeding customers while keeping costs under control. To be an effective leader in the theater industry, he learned cost control and all aspects of theater operations (securing staff, training them well, making sure they dressed appropriately and knew how to treat customers, maintaining a clean environment, and more). Barry also complimented his job at Lucas & Jenkins by becoming involved in his new community. He took part in the development of Macon Little Theatre and was elected in 1934 as the first treasurer of the new organization.

Though he was establishing a presence in his new hometown, in his earliest months in Macon, Art Barry was drawn back to Lakeland, Florida almost every weekend. Following the final show on Saturday nights, Barry drove down US Highway 41 and over to the central Florida city to court his sweetheart and future bride, Texas Roughton. They married soon after he moved to Georgia and settled in to raise a family in Macon.

As City Manager for Lucas & Jenkins Theatres, Barry certainly crossed paths with Leonard Berg during the years. He probably dined at Berg's restaurant between duties at the Capitol on Second Street and the Rialto on Cherry. He may have stopped for lunch or dinner before heading over to the Grand on Mulberry to check on his staff. In 1939, the two men collaborated to include advertising for Berg's cafe on cards promoting current movies at Barry's theaters. Perhaps their association gave Leonard Berg a glimpse of the movie house manager's work ethic and his success in business.

In 1943, when Berg decided it was time to retire, the United States was immersed in a second World War. Food rationing, gas rationing, men gone to war, price freezes, and labor shortages added to the stress of operating a restaurant, something Berg had been doing his entire adult life. He sold his business to Art and Texas Barry, then worked with the new owners for just one week before walking away. Barry and Berg managed to maintain their friendship through occasional visits at Berg's home on Nottingham Drive.

At the time of the change in ownership, Len Berg's Cafe served only about 100 customers a day, perhaps related to economic struggles associated with the war. The Barrys arrived in the business in time to see the government decree that patrons no longer needed to use ration coupons for restaurant meals. The end of the war further eased restrictions on food and gas, the economy began to improve, and the restaurant industry was poised to rise to new levels. As author John Mariani stated in *America Eats Out*, "With the end of the war, the restaurant industry in America was set for the biggest boom in its history, and it drew on the services of millions of returning GI's to man its kitchens and counters, improve its efficiency, and expand its possibilities as the population exploded."

Barry began shaping the restaurant staff with his own style of management and faced the potential for growth in his business without most of the cooks who had worked with Berg. To ensure he knew how to lead the kitchen as well as service staff, Barry went home at the end of each day and spent hours in the kitchen training himself to prepare food as he expected his staff to do. Texas scrubbed pots and cleaned the stove behind him and offered cooking advice as needed.

Earlier, in his youth, Barry dove into the movie industry by reading his brother's books on the subject. Shifting to a new industry, he had similar resources available to study, with texts such as Duncan Hines's *Adventures in Good Cooking* or *Wenzel's Menu Maker*. Barry knew well from movie goers that customers expected clean floors and friendly service, and he was not surprised that Hines stressed the importance of consistent quality and a clean environment. The new restaurateur had experience with training staff to cater to customers in a manner that satisfied but left them hungry to return. He knew about

managing costs and overhead and learned from the Wenzel's publication how that translated to managing a restaurant.

One of the first tasks Barry faced was doing an inventory of the food, equipment, and supplies Berg left behind. Among the pots and pans and plates, he found hundreds of cases of empty beer bottles, and though he was not interested in serving alcoholic beverages, Barry understood some customers might want something with their meal other than iced tea or a strong cup of Savarin coffee. He called on a local Schlitz distributor who agreed to come and collect the empty bottles in exchange for Barry's business. That business might have been slower than the Schlitz distributor expected, since Barry sold beer only to customers who ordered a meal. Under its new owner, Len Berg's used less than a case of beer each week.

Food sales increased, and Barry maintained Berg's high standards for the coffee and iced tea he served. He kept menu favorites like "Steak in the Red" (a half-pound beef tenderloin filet with chili on top), chop suey, and Italian spaghetti. Art Barry also heeded the advice he found in industry publications and introduced new dishes like "Crab Meat Remick," "Celery Au Gratin," and "Hamburger Steak."

Jeff Amerson and Wilbur Mitcham (c. 1960).

A Second Helping

As he fine-tuned the menu, Barry found at one point he had more than eighty items on the a-la-carte menu. Striving for efficiency as well as customer satisfaction, he began to pare the number down. In order to streamline the ordering process, Barry implemented a new system so the staff could quickly communicate about what the customer wanted. On the menu, a letter of the alphabet introduced each entree and vegetable selection. As patrons placed their orders from the menu, waiters and waitresses jotted down the single letter and delivered a ticket to the kitchen staff. Even though the menu changed daily, the cooks, many of whom could not read, easily identified which items to dish onto the plate. A pattern evolved so the menu noted the fish of the day with an X, the poultry dish was labeled with a C, and cole slaw or carrot & raisin salad was designated by a Z.

The kitchen staff's literacy was not as important to Barry as their ability to consistently prepare good food. Food critic Hines once wrote that food in many American eateries was so bad, it was clear it had been prepared by chefs who had no idea what they were doing; he suggested it was cooked by men who simply needed a job. Art Barry took on the restaurant business at a time when a lot of men, servicemen returning from the war, were seeking employment. He hired one veteran in 1946 who clearly countered Hines' observations. Barry's new cook definitely knew his way around the kitchen.

Wilbur Mitcham was hired as a short-order cook at Len Berg's, and within a short time, he became the lead chef. Mitcham had studied with an Asian chef in New York City for a while, but he had also been involved in restaurants since the age of twelve. All the other cooks—Mary Dee, Annette, Irene, and others-knew what they were doing, too, but Mitcham helped organize duties so each person knew how to fill in at another station if necessary. He helped ensure the kitchen staff met Barry's standards and kept the recipes consistent, no matter who stirred the pot on any given day.

Barry also recruited another veteran to his restaurant shortly after the young man was discharged from service and returned to Macon. Jeff Amerson had worked with Barry at Lucas & Jenkins, and briefly at Len Berg's, before he went into the Army. The restaurant owner hired Amerson in 1945 and soon appointed him to the role of Assistant Manager.

Unlike Berg, Barry delegated management tasks and organized his staff so he did not have to close the eatery if he was unable to be there. Harold Norris was general manager for many years, and he was responsible for overall operations when Barry was not present. Assistant manager Amerson helped Norris greet customers, receive supplies, and coordinate with Mitcham to ensure the kitchen ran smoothly. Managers and owner picked up dishes or bus pans, if needed, and worked long hours to keep the business operating through lunch and dinner.

Each day, as advised by the *Wenzel's Menu Maker* on the shelf in his office, Barry and his managers inventoried stock and ran tickets to monitor sales. Monday through Saturday, Barry, his managers, and staff made

Waitresses receive camellias to brighten the season. Photo courtesy of Middle Georgia Archives, Washington Memorial Library, Macon, Georgia.

sure the house was clean and ready for the next meal. Sunday was the only day Len Berg's did not serve customers, but even then, there was work to be done at the Wall Street diner.

The work paid off, and Barry was delighted to see his business grow right along with Macon's population. The 1950 census counted 100,000 residents, an increase of 30,000 from ten years earlier. Many new residents arrived with the military and support installations during the war (Camp Wheeler, Cochran Field, Naval Ordinance Plant, and more). Others came to take advantage of the more than 16,000 industrial jobs that existed in Macon in 1949.

The growing community continued to find Len Berg's across the alley from Union Dry Goods (which soon became Davison's Department Store). Other retail shops, like Burden Smith on Second Street and Kress's Dime Store on Cherry, brought shoppers to enjoy lunch at Barry's establishment, and office workers from Cotton Avenue, Broadway, or Poplar Street often walked over for a meal.

Downtown bustled with activity in the evening as well. The theaters Barry had managed for Lucas & Jenkins continued to thrive, and the Grand even hosted the world premier of a Hollywood movie. (The Grand, originally built in 1883 and 1884 as the Academy of Music, had become a movie house in 1936, around the time Barry moved to Macon. It functioned in that role until 1965, when the last movie shown there was *The Sound of Music*.) In February 1945 the community followed the spotlight to the Grand, where Robert L. Scott and other guests celebrated the opening of *God is My Co-Pilot*, a movie based on Scott's book of the same name. It recounted the Macon native's experience with the Flying Tigers during World War II.

On any given night, theaters spread throughout the city still saw crowds of moviegoers, people celebrating the new postwar economy and taking advantage of the social networking opportunities of the day. Dates often included a dinner out before attending a movie, and though it was not as formal as the Colony in Manhattan or the Pump Room in Chicago, Len Berg's offered Maconites a comfortable atmosphere. Couples or small parties could enjoy a good meal in the restaurant's private dining rooms. Diners in a rush could order their meal at the counter instead of waiting for a table. College students from Mercer or Wesleyan escaped campus to dine in the alley, getting a good meal to satisfy their appetites and their mothers' concerns about nutrition.

Five years after purchasing Len Berg's, Barry suffered a setback. On Friday, August 13, 1948, a crowd of about thirty diners were swept out of the building when fire broke out in the kitchen. Barry had left the business in the capable hands of his night manager, Jeff Amerson. Amerson and Chef Wilbur Mitcham ushered customers and personnel out of the building while Macon firefighters battled the blaze for an hour or more. Fire and water damage was estimated in the thousands of dollars.

Barry told reporters he would begin repair work as soon as possible, and he suggested he might set up business in a temporary location. The following January, the *Macon Telegraph* announced Len Berg's new restaurant would open in the Terminal Station. According to the article, "The former stand in Wall Street Alley closed Friday night [December 31, 1948] after 15 years in that location. (Family members could not recall details about how, or even if, Len Berg's operated between the time of the fire in August and the end of the year.)

The *Macon Telegraph* announced the new operation at Macon's railroad hub and described Len Berg's at the Terminal Station as having a renovated lunchroom, concession and cigar stands in the station lobby, and the separate "Booker T. Restaurant for Negroes."

Jeff Amerson and Harold Norris at Len Berg's during its operation in the Terminal Station (1949)

Though in earlier decades as many as a hundred trains would arrive and depart daily from the Terminal Station, by 1949 those were being displaced by automobile and airplane travel. But trains still provided convenient transportation from coastal Georgia to the capitol in Atlanta, and Macon was an important hub along the way. The location seemed ideal for a bustling food business. Barry's son A.P. "Buster" Barry, Jr., recalled that in addition to serving customers on-site in the various stands in the station, Len Berg's was also required to provide food service to passengers and railroad workers coming through on trains. Buster remembered helping his mother and Amerson peddle sandwiches and drinks to customers on board the Nancy Hanks and other trains that passed through the city.

Len Berg's did not benefit from the move to the Terminal Station. The dining experience in the cavernous building could not offer the ambience of private dining rooms that were part of the little building Berg and League had designed. Barry also thought the people of Macon were intrigued by the restaurant's location in the alley. He wanted to move back, and Buster Barry and Celia Amerson recalled that he did so after only a few months at the Terminal Station.

Barry had to know, however, that a return to Wall Street was not a permanent solution to his restaurant operations. Automobiles were becoming more and more prevalent and parking was becoming an issue. Also, sometime in the fall of 1948 (perhaps after the fire) Woolworth's Department Store leased property on Cherry Street, the site formerly occupied by Kress's Department Store. The new lease designated the entire tract of property from Cherry Street to Wall Street, including where the fire-damaged Len Berg's Restaurant sat. Barry had to seek another location and figure a way to replicate the successful charm of the restaurant in the alley.

Two years after the fire, in August 1950, Arthur and Texas Barry secured a site, one

A Second Helping

Managers Jeff Amerson, Harold Norris, Attorney Arthur Lewis, and Contractor W.A. Stillwell Jr. watch Mayor Lewis B. Wilson place an envelope in the cornerstone of the restaurant's new building (August 1950). Photo courtesy of Middle Georgia Archives, Washington Memorial Library, Macon, Georgia.

that allowed for parking to accommodate the increased number of patrons who drove downtown to dine. The Barrys signed a twenty-year ground lease with Mrs. George Smith, Sr., for a lot that was a block north of the original restaurant on Wall Street. Though the location for the new Len Berg's Restaurant was to be diagonally across from the Federal Courthouse at the intersection of Third Street Lane and Walnut Street Lane, the location was generally known as the Post Office Alley.

Using the familiar drawings done by Ellamae Ellis League, W.A. Stillwell Jr., the original contractor of the Wall Street building, started construction immediately after the Barrys secured the lease. Macon Mayor Lewis B. Wilson marked the occasion by placing an envelope in the cornerstone of the new building as Stillwell, Arthur Lewis, Jeff Amerson, and Harold Norris stood by to watch. The envelope contained a current menu, several recipes, and a copy of Lewis's history of the restaurant.

Stillwell recycled doors, counters, windows, and other fixtures from the original Wall Street building. Barry directed Stillwell to use opaque glass in the large windows by the front door instead of clear panes. (Sometime before 1969, the opaque glass was replaced with multicolored cathedral glass that became a signature feature of Len Berg's.)

The new building maintained small, private dining rooms on each side of the building, complete with slatted swinging doors and a bell so patrons could ring for their server. Years later, when they removed the privacy doors, Barry installed bells by the exit doors in the front halls. Teenagers Patsy and Buster Barry scratched their initials into the concrete sidewalk to mark completion of the building, and Len Berg's Restaurant opened in its new location in October 1950.

Celebrating with a good meal. Photo courtesy of Middle Georgia Archives, Washington Memorial Library, Macon, Georgia.

A Second Helping

The restaurant became part of the changing landscape around Walnut and Ocmulgee Streets. (Between 1888 and 1951, the street running parallel to the river between Seventh Street and Orange Street was known as Ocmulgee Street. Before 1888, it was identified as Wharf Street, and after 1951, it became Riverside Drive.) At the time the Barrys began construction of the restaurant, the building was located behind the Smiths' house that faced Walnut Street. Their neighbors across Third Street Lane were the Howard Johnsons. The tree-shaded residences along Walnut would eventually make way for commercial and professional enterprises.

Through the years after the Barrys purchased the restaurant from Leonard Berg, Texas occasionally took her children there for a meal. Patsy and Buster grew up knowing about their father's business, and by the time he scratched his initials in the sidewalk of the new building, Buster Barry had begun to work at the restaurant part-time. His father and assistant manager Amerson guided young Buster through various jobs: bussing tables, washing dishes, doing inventory. Buster delayed going into business full time in order to start college at Georgia Tech in 1954.

With his son busy at college, the senior Barry named a new manager for Len Berg's. Jeff

Amerson had already worked with him for more than ten years, during which time they had developed an extraordinary bond. Buster Barry, who was a child when Amerson started at Len Berg's, marveled at how his father and Amerson knew each other so well. They could finish one another's stories—like one about a dead mule in the bathtub or another one about a sow and wheelbarrow. Buster noted with admiration, "Jeff was the man." He recalled that although his father owned the restaurant, it was Jeff Amerson who ran it. "When Jeff was there, Len Berg's ran like a Swiss watch."

The year Buster graduated from Georgia Tech in 1958, Len Berg's celebrated a milestone. A special golden anniversary dinner menu highlighted the fifty years the restaurant had operated in Macon. It featured items Berg would have served during his tenure: sea foods, steaks and chops, Chinese foods, Italian dishes. The ever-popular filet mignon steak—served with potatoes, bread, and butter—was priced at $1.75, or diners could order eggs and omelets with half a ham steak for $1.25. For those who wanted to splurge, Len Berg's offered a large T-bone steak for $4.50.

Sometime prior to the 1958 golden anniversary, Art Barry added a special dessert that would become one of Len Berg's Restaurant signature dishes. Various theories abound about the origins of "Macaroon Pie." One story suggests that Barry tasted the crunchy pie when he was on a fishing trip in Florida; another claimed a customer who dined in Miami at the Fontainebleu Resort Hotel (which held its Grand Opening in 1954) recommended Barry give it a try; a recipe that appeared in the 1957 issue of Duncan Hines's *Adventures in Good Cooking* may have inspired Barry to add the delicacy to his menu. But whatever its origins, "Macaroon Pie" became closely associated with the Len Berg's name.

Minding tradition and keeping familiar favorites were important to the identity of the restaurant, but Art Barry was certainly not opposed to experimenting with recipes and trying new dishes he thought his customers might enjoy. When his son, Buster, graduated from Georgia Tech and flew as a navigator in the Navy, Barry and his wife, Texas, visited their son in Hawaii. There, the senior Barry found he could purchase macadamia chips at a fraction of the cost of pecans back home. At his son's apartment, Barry experimented with his signature dessert, and the results were delicious. He ordered a large quantity of nut chips to ship back to Georgia, and the cooks at Len Berg's used macadamia chips in the macaroon pie until the price of local pecans returned to normal.

The younger Barry finished his service with the Navy in 1962, and he and his wife, Carolyn, returned to Macon with a two-year-old son, A.P. Barry III. Buster worked with his father and Jeff Amerson, a man who had been like a big brother to him. The young Barry was inducted into the restaurant business full time: he assisted in managing staff, payroll and overhead, purchasing and receiving; he learned about recipe control, portion control, and guest check control. One of the earliest and strongest lessons about restaurant management came from observing his father's and Amerson's diligence about controlling food costs. "We might serve fourteen cases of chicken in a week, but if one chicken was missing from the inventory, they figured out where the loss occurred."

With the goal of keeping food costs at or below thirty percent of total operational costs, Len Berg's management took daily inventory seriously. The data collected also told them which dishes were most successful.

Manager Jeff Amerson with kitchen and wait staff. Chef Wilbur Mitcham is standing in the back row, far right. (1950)

In his earliest days as an assistant manager, Buster convinced his father to let him design a marketing campaign around a new menu item he wanted to try. Buster had traveled to Hawaii, Japan, and the Pacific Islands, and he thought Len Berg's customers might enjoy meals from that region of the world, where rice was an important staple. He came up with a simple advertisement promoting his idea: Rice is Nice. The day after the new ad appeared in the local newspaper, Buster beamed when he saw they had sold two orders of his new menu offering. However, when he compared the day's sales figures to the meticulous records his father kept on all food sales, Buster discovered they sold about two orders of rice every time it was offered on the menu, whether it was part of a new Asian dish or with tomatoes or beef tips.

As Amerson and Barry recorded sales and checked on leftover food every day, they pored over figures to determine the cost of individual ingredients. While Amerson used an adding machine, the senior Barry scribbled notes on the back of an old menu. The senior Barry often announced the food cost to the penny before Amerson could even finish his calculations on the machine. Buster Barry recalled a time when his father challenged Amerson to determine the cost of oil to fry a single order of shrimp or oysters. Amerson worked diligently with the kitchen staff, measuring the oil before and after they fried an order of seafood. He determined they used one-half of a teaspoon of oil each time and calculated the cost of that portion of the oil they ordered. When it came time to print new menus, Barry was confident about the new price he charged for fried shrimp.

Increasing a price was not something Art Barry did lightly. When he had to raise the price of "Minced Steak" from ninety-five cents to a dollar, the restaurant owner did not sleep for a week. He worried no one would want to order the popular entree at the increased price. He tried, at first, to adjust the portion size, but that was tricky too. He wanted to be sure the serving was just right—large enough to satisfy the customer at a cost they could swallow and priced so the cost met his thirty percent food cost goal. The owner wanted customers to recall his food was so delicious they cleaned their plate, and yet he wanted them to leave room for dessert.

Like any good restaurateur, Barry monitored how much leftover food went into the garbage pail, because this indicated either the kitchen was putting too much food on the plate or there was a problem with the taste or quality. There were not often complaints about the quality of food, but Buster Barry recalled one customer's issue about portion sizes.

It came from a regular customer, family friend Arthur Lewis, who often brought his wife and daughter to dinner after closing his office on Cherry Street. One hot summer night, Lewis asked if the younger Barry knew why the owner had recently installed air conditioning in the restaurant. Buster reasoned that his father wanted to keep customers cool and happy, but Lewis countered with a laugh and said, "Hell, no! It's because they cut the pork chops so thin those big cooling fans in the kitchen kept blowing 'em off the plate!"

It took only a moment for Buster to realize his friend was joking, and he enjoyed such humor because it was a welcome relief in the "interesting environment" and stressful work associated with operating a restaurant. Everyone worked hard and seemed content, and though Amerson and his father made the complex business look simple, Buster noted "The food had to be bought right, cooked right, and served right."

Even the senior Barry managed to cook up some occasional mischief to keep things light. Once, when thunderstorms threatened to disrupt their day's operations, the owner and his manager plotted some fun. Amerson grabbed a large empty Wesson Oil can and took his position by the door into the kitchen; Barry stepped into place by the exit door on the other side of the counter.

According to plan, Amerson banged on the tin can at the same time Barry flipped off the lights. Amerson got the biggest kick out of their prank as he watched the cooks and dishwashers scatter—right over the top of their boss!

Buster Barry recalled hearing his father and Amerson tell about the incident for years, and realizing his father could laugh at his own foibles made it easier to take when the laughter was directed at younger members of the family. Years after retiring from a successful business career, Buster remembered his father's teasing about an early lesson in customer service.

Buster admired the ease with which his father and Jeff Amerson greeted customers. They could make total strangers feel like part of the family and make them feel welcome. When he returned from the Navy and went to work full time, Buster was anxious to model their behavior, and he looked for ways to say something to each new customer to make them feel special, so they would know he welcomed them, too.

One day, when a group of Macon socialites entered the restaurant, Buster cleared his throat and went to work. He recognized one of the women, remembering he had recently met her charming daughter. Buster recalled hearing how the girl had created the floral centerpiece and prepared appetizers for the party; his wife, Carolyn, was impressed because the young woman had made the beautiful dress she was wearing. Buster thought of the young girl's homemaking skills and complimented his customer before he directed the group to a seat out front while they waited for a table. Feeling pleased about welcoming such a distinguished group of ladies, Buster excused himself and went about his other duties.

During the lunch rush, it was not unusual for one person to greet a party and another to show them to a table. On this occasion, it was the senior Barry who seated the group of ladies. Shortly after, when they had an opportunity to talk, Barry asked his son what he said when he greeted the group. Puzzled by the question, Buster explained how he and Carolyn had recently met the woman's daughter. He had told the woman so, and complimented her on having such a "homely" girl who would make a good wife for someone some day.

Art Barry simply nodded his head. "Did you, now?"

At the end of that particular busy day, Buster went to his usual station in Room 6 to run the day's tickets. There, on the table, he found a large dictionary—the one that usually sat next to *Wenzel's Menu Maker* and the *Macon City Directory* on the shelf in the office. It was open to a page in the middle, and it took a moment for Buster to find his vocabulary lesson for the day. At first, the young man was relieved his father had not lectured or teased him about the verbal gaffe, until he realized everyone who worked at Len Berg's now knew the meaning of "homely."

Vocabulary lessons—especially those that affected customers—were not limited to young, new hosts. Buster remembered once when Jeff Amerson tried to deliver a lesson to one of Len Berg's long-time waitresses. He overheard her asking a new customer if he wanted another dinner roll, and Amerson tried to explain to Miss V how some people might interpret that as her way of saying they were eating too much.

Miss V, even as she neared retirement age, was an efficient waitress with many loyal customers. Still, Amerson was concerned that new customers might not appreciate her brusque nature or might be offended by her style of service. He quietly took the waitress aside and explained the subtle difference in how he wanted her to approach the situation. "Don't ask if the customer wants another roll. You should simply ask if they would like a roll."

Amerson and his young assistant manager were surprised when Miss V handled the criticism without her usual grumbling. Before the day was over, they even heard the veteran waitress ask one of her regulars if he wanted "a roll" just as she had been coached to do. Before Buster could congratulate Amerson on his success, though, Miss V put her hand on her hip and drawled, "Well, then, would you like another corn stick?"

The waitress may have handled her reprimand with her own brand of subtlety, not something she was known for. Usually, Miss V grumbled loudly and slammed things around, letting everyone around her know when she was unhappy. On one such occasion, a loyal customer smiled as he put his tip on the counter and told Amerson, "I think I'd best go before the squash starts flying!"

The customer, a banker who dined at the counter almost every day, listened to Miss V talk about retirement one day after Barry suggested it was time for her to give up being a waitress. As she pondered what to do, the banker asked if she had something in mind. "Well, I think I'd like to work in a bank like you do. I could sit in one of those dark offices up front and stare out at the lobby all day long, just like you do."

The banker almost fell off the stool laughing —and Miss V served up another roll.

Customers like the banker and Arthur Lewis, who joked about thin pork chops blowing away, were part of the Len Berg's family. They were among the hundreds of people served each day, and they were willing to find humor amid the hustle and bustle of the busy restaurant. Occasionally, though, humor backfired.

Buster Barry recalled an angry customer who rushed back in from the parking lot and growled, "What kind of dump are y'all running here?" The irate man reported his new car had been stolen while he was having lunch, and Art Barry walked up as the man provided details for the manager to report to police. Upon hearing, "It was a brand new Nash!" Barry offered his condolences and said, "Well, just sit here a minute. I'm sure they'll bring it right back."

The stranger was not amused by the owner's comment, but others nearby enjoyed a good laugh. They might have held a similar opinion of the brand of stolen car, or they understood Barry's wry sense of humor. Regular customers knew the restaurant owner was likely to turn the joke on himself or his staff, too. Many remembered when Barry and Jeff Amerson joined forces to tease their night manager, J.D. Smith, about a statement he had made on local television. Smith, or Smitty, as he was known by most in the community, was a fire inspector who worked as a night manager at Len Berg's. He was on call when fire struck the historic Wesleyan Conservatory in 1963, and he spoke to a local news reporter about the massive fire that destroyed the original Wesleyan College building and three apartments.

The next day, Amerson and Barry corralled Smitty in the front hall with a familiar group of diners who wanted to hear about the fire. "So," Amerson asked, after reminding the group of Smitty's televised explanation, "how long did it take you to figure out it was either arson or an accident? What else could it have been?"

Of course, Amerson was not immune to teasing, either, especially with the Pallbearers around. The group of six men met each month for lunch at Len Berg's and claimed they added new members only when one of their group died and they needed a new pallbearer to help carry the load. At one of their monthly meetings, Barry primed the group before inviting Amerson to Room 3 to tell them about the business course he had recently started. "Now, let me get this straight," Barry slapped his manager on the shoulder and held him in place. "You were taking a course to improve your memory,

right? But you can't finish the course because you don't remember where you left your textbook?"

Either Amerson's memory lapse was a joke or he learned a lot before he lost the textbook. Amerson rarely forgot anything and claimed that he "remembered for the elephants." He rarely had to jot down notes about what supplies he needed to order or to remember the order in which customers entered.

Keeping tabs on which customers to seat next was important to the restaurant's success, especially since Barry maintained Berg's policy of first come, first served. It became even more important as the community faced upheaval during the civil

Manager Jeff Amerson (c. 1962)

A Second Helping

rights movement of the 1960s. It had to be clear to everyone that Len Berg's Restaurant had a policy that was fair to all.

Like many restaurants in the South, Len Berg's employed African-American cooks, as well as dishwashers and busboys and waiters. They were important employees who helped keep the business running, but employees sat at a table to eat only after customers were gone for the day. The same was true for all staff, but the difference in many restaurants was that individuals who were black were not welcome to dine as customers in those same establishments.

With the news that local businesses were being tested for their tolerance to desegregation, Barry called in his managers to clarify his restaurant's policy on seating black customers. Amerson—a son of the rural South, who was named after the president of the Confederacy—got along well with all of the staff, but he had never been in the position of serving a customer who was African-American. He expressed no opposition to seating all customers, and neither did the younger Barry. Art Barry directed his son and Amerson to meet with the staff to explain the restaurant's seating policy.

First, the managers brought in the kitchen staff and then the wait staff to state that Len Berg's Restaurant had a house rule to serve all customers who came through the doors, regardless of the color of their skin. The policy directive had little effect on or reaction from the kitchen staff—the cooks would continue to prepare the same quality foods they always had. Waiters (all of whom were African-American) and waitresses reacted with greater concern. Their livelihood depended on tips, and many worried about the impact desegregation might have on business, and in turn, on their income. One waiter voiced his worry. "If the wrong folks come in and start trouble, then nobody will want to come here to eat." Another waiter echoed the concern and loudly protested the "we serve everyone" policy.

Barry was not swayed by the service staff's concern.

The same evening, after Amerson and young Barry met with Len Berg's staff, the second waiter—the one who protested loudest about Barry's policy on desegregation—became Len Berg's Restaurant first African-American customer. Accompanied by a bevy of ladies on his arm, the waiter appeared to exude a sense of unseemly satisfaction as he directed Amerson to seat his party in Room 3. Amerson seated the group, and they were served without incidence, but the relationship between the two men was strained afterwards. Amerson has suggested it was not the fact he had to serve a black man, but rather, it was more about the way the man haughtily presented himself after voicing disdain for Barry's proclamation.

Within a few days, Barry's "we serve everyone" policy was tested again, this time by strangers. Two men, one white and the other African-American, entered the busy restaurant at noon. They requested a seat at the lunch counter, the most visible seating in the house. Though it was a new situation for everyone in the crowded eatery, the men received the same courtesy and respect dished out to every customer. They enjoyed a meal at one of Macon's signature restaurants, and the important desegregation "firsts" for Len Berg's were history. It took a while for such actions to become non-events in the community, but Len Berg's did not suffer an apparent loss of clientele because of their tolerance.

Much of the community was still trying to cope with social changes at this time, and much as it had been for Camp Wheeler residents in the days of World War II, the 1960s was a period when Macon's Mercer University and Wesleyan College closely monitored their students' whereabouts. Parents often expected colleges to place restrictions on social activities, to help keep the young people safe when they were far from home and the watchful eye of parents. "Wesleyan Girls" faced restrictions on what social activities were deemed appropriate. To sign out of the dorm, they had to go with a group or an approved escort, and they had to designate their destination.

The young women who attended Wesleyan enjoyed the booming popularity of rhythm and blues music as much as teens everywhere else in the country. Though black musicians often performed in Macon, such concerts were not deemed an appropriate destination for Wesleyan Girls. But they knew where to go to hear all about the performances. After Otis Redding performed at the Douglass Theater or James Brown had been in town to perform, the girls planned a night out to Len Berg's. They waited for a seat with their favorite waiter, then ordered the Satellite Special (a filet mignon, baked potato and salad for $1.98) and the latest scoop from their waiter, Swanson.

Art Barry had sent his own son, Buster, to college in Atlanta, visited him when the young man was in the Navy, and saw him return home to Macon to work in the family business. The younger Barry enjoyed much of his work, especially interacting with customers once he grew more comfortable with his greetings. The work he enjoyed most, though, was any opportunity to run errands away from the confines of the restaurant. He preferred being out. Rather than weighing and inventorying cold food from the cooler, Buster wanted to cruise through the Farmers' Market to buy produce.

In the middle part of the 1960s, Art Barry opened a new operation that seemed to suit his son's needs to be on the move. Len Berg's Food to Go opened on Ingleside Avenue, and Buster Barry was named manager for the new style of restaurant. The eatery served the same foods as Len Berg's—food that was prepared in the kitchen downtown—but it focused on sending meals out instead of having customers dine in. New Styrofoam containers made it possible to dish up food and keep it warm for a while, long enough for customers to drive home from the restaurant and deliver a healthy meal to the family.

Buster enjoyed the relative freedom of the "to-go" dining concept, and in 1969 he made a very personal decision to separate his business from his father's restaurant. Art Barry supported his plans, and Buster partnered with Albert Guest to start Pick-Up Meals by Barry. The operation was independent from Len Berg's, but the menu continued to offer familiar entrees and Southern standards such as fried corn, collards, and butter beans. Buster had a familiar cook on his staff, and he used lessons learned about rotating selections to keep customers happy. He and Guest opened their first shop on Pio Nono Avenue, and added several more locations before Buster branched out to still another career. He maintained shares in Pick-Up Meals until 1991, but many years before that, Buster Barry joined forces with Guy Eberhardt to start a commercial real estate business. When he retired after years in his own restaurant and a career in real estate, Buster claimed that his nighttime dreams were always about his time at Len Berg's, and "they were always the most pleasant kind of memories."

When Art Barry decided to retire, he knew his son had carved out a successful career of his own. In November 1969 Art and Texas Barry passed the torch of Len Berg's Restaurant to another young man they felt they had practically raised, Jefferson Davis Amerson.

Arthur P. Barry congratulates Jeff Amerson on his purchase of Len Berg's (1969). Photo courtesy of Middle Georgia Archives, Washington Memorial Library, Macon, Georgia.

RECIPES FROM THE BARRY ERA

Minced Steak with Brown Gravy

Crabmeat Remick

Butter-Baked Quarter Chicken

Pork Chops Hawaiian

Celery au Gratin

Salad Dressings

Macaroon Pie

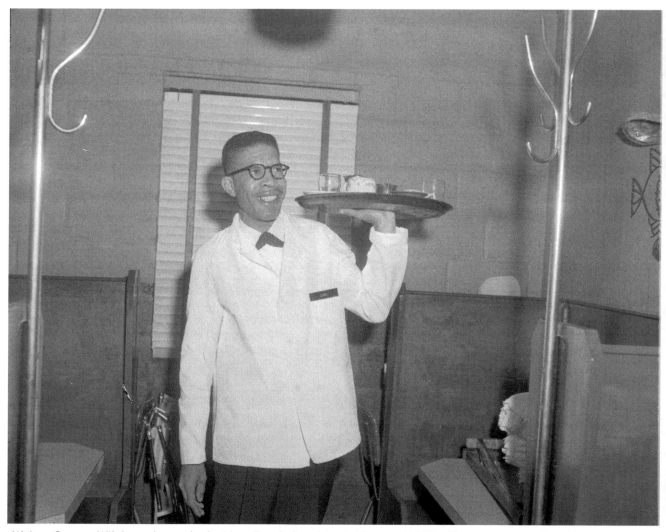

Waiter George Wilcher who worked at Len Berg's for almost 40 years (1960). Photo courtesy of Middle Georgia Archives, Washington Memorial Library, Macon, Georgia.

A Second Helping

Minced Steak with Brown Gravy

Art Barry bought Len Berg's Restaurant in the early 1940s, at a time when America was embroiled in World War II. The era came with wartime challenges that included food rationing, and restaurateurs had to stretch ingredients just as cooks at home did. A popular dish at the time—and one that continued to be a favorite for another sixty years—was minced steak. Sometimes, the menu identified it as "Minced Steak with Brown Gravy"; other times, it was listed as "Minced Steak with Mushroom Gravy."

DIRECTIONS

Mix together 1 to 2 pounds of ground chuck, a beaten egg, salt, pepper, and crushed saltines; form into patties. Cook on a flat grill until done.

The gravy is a mixture of beef stock thickened with cornstarch. Add a small can of mushrooms to the gravy and stir in a spoonful of Gravy Master* to add color and additional flavor to the gravy.

Place several minced steaks into the pan of gravy and keep on the steam table or in an oven to keep warm until serving.

*Gravy Master is a seasoning and browning sauce used to add flavor and color to gravies, stews, sauces, etc. You can purchase the product or make your own by heating ½ cup sugar in a saucepan over low to medium-low heat until it is browned (about 5 to 10 minutes). When the sugar starts to get dark, remove it from the heat and **carefully** add one cup hot water. (This step causes the mixture to pop and sputter, so be careful!) Add beef base and put back on a low heat; stir until everything is dissolved. Cool and store in a disposable container.

MINCED STEAK WITH BROWN GRAVY

INGREDIENTS

1 to 2 lbs. ground chuck

egg

salt and pepper, to taste

saltines

Gravy:

beef stock

cornstarch

canned mushrooms

Gravy Master*

Crabmeat Remick

CRABMEAT REMICK

INGREDIENTS

2 C. (1 lb.) cooked crabmeat

butter

6 slices bacon

1 tsp. dry mustard

½ tsp. paprika

½ tsp. celery salt

2 drops Tabasco

1 tsp. tarragon vinegar

1 ¾ C. mayonnaise

1/2 C. chili sauce

Just as his predecessor Berg did, Art Barry mixed new dishes with traditional favorites. He introduced this seafood entree to Len Berg's diners in the 1950s.

Directions

Preheat oven to 400 degrees. Pick over 2 cups (about 1 pound) of cooked crab meat to remove shells. Butter six individual casseroles or ramekins. Fry 6 slices of bacon until crisp.

In a small bowl, combine 1 teaspoon dry mustard with ½ teaspoon paprika and ½ teaspoon celery salt. Add these dry ingredients along with 2 drops of Tabasco, and 1 teaspoon tarragon vinegar to 1 ¾ cups of mayonnaise. Add ½ cup chili sauce. Mix in the crabmeat and divide into the six ramekins. Bake for 15 minutes or until the sauce bubbles. Top with bacon strip and return to oven to brown.

Butter-baked Quarter Chicken

Years after Buster Barry left Len Berg's Restaurant, he still remembered how to prepare the Butter-Baked Quarter Chicken; Jerry Amerson recalled the process, too. Both men described the recipe much the same as Len Berg's cooks would have: put together the ingredients you want and cook for as long as needed. It worked for them, but here's a bit more detail.

DIRECTIONS

Preheat oven to 350 degrees.

Wash and pat dry a quarter of a chicken. Salt and pepper to taste, then dredge in flour. Add to a roasting pan or 13- x 9-inch baking dish with ½ inch of hot water in which you've dissolved about a teaspoon of "chicken base" or chicken bouillon. Pour ¼ cup melted butter over the top, cover the pan with foil, and put in hot oven to bake until almost done (about 35 minutes). Stir in a small amount of cornstarch to thicken the liquid, add a drop or two of yellow food coloring, and leave the pan uncovered to bake another 30 minutes.

BUTTER-BAKED QUARTER CHICKEN

INGREDIENTS

¼ chicken

salt and pepper, to taste

flour

hot water

1 tsp. chicken bouillon

¼ C. melted butter

cornstarch

PORK CHOPS HAWAIIAN

INGREDIENTS

pork chops (4 oz. each)

salt and pepper, to taste

2 C. water

4 Tbsp. soy sauce

3 Tbsp. vinegar

3 Tbsp. brown sugar

pineapple slices

rice

Art and Texas Barry visited their son, Buster, when his Navy service took him to Hawaii. This recipe might have been a result of their visit, or it might have been introduced when Buster tried his "Rice is Nice" ad campaign.

Directions

Preheat oven to 350 degrees.

Fill a flat pan (13- x 21-inch) with several 4-ounce pork chops; salt and pepper to taste. Add 2 cups of water and cook in oven until done (about 20-25 minutes). Add 4 tablespoons of soy sauce, 3 tablespoons of vinegar, and sprinkle with 3 tablespoons of brown sugar. Put a slice of pineapple on top of each chop and return to the oven to cook until the pineapple is browned. Serve with rice.

Celery Au Gratin

This was a dish Buster Barry recalled from his years of working with his father and Jeff Amerson.

DIRECTIONS

Cut and parboil several stalks of celery until tender; drain.

Prepare a cream sauce of 2 tablespoons butter, 2 tablespoons flour, salt and pepper to taste, 1 cup chicken stock, and ½ cup light cream.

Butter 1 cup bread crumbs (drench with melted butter), and put ¼ cup in the bottom of a baking dish. Layer half the celery, another ¼ cup of the crumbs, and sprinkle with ¼ cup shredded cheddar cheese. Add the remaining celery and pour the cream sauce over the mix. Add another ¼ cup shredded cheddar and the remaining bread crumbs.

Place in hot oven and bake 30 minutes or until heated through and the crumbs are brown.

CELERY AU GRATIN

INGREDIENTS

celery stalks

~~~~

Cream sauce:

2 Tbsp. butter

2 Tbsp. flour

salt and pepper, to taste

1 C. chicken stock

½ C. light cream

~~~~

1 C. bread crumbs

melted butter

½ C. shredded cheddar cheese, divided in half

Salad Dressings

SALAD DRESSINGS

INGREDIENTS

Epic dressing:

2 C. ketchup

1 ½ C. Wesson oil

½ C. apple cider vinegar

⅓ C. sugar

2 tsp. pepper

2 tsp. salt

4 tsp. paprika

Salads made with iceberg lettuce began to appear on American menus in the 1950s, initially as a simple wedge of lettuce, and then later tossed with tomatoes, cucumbers, and other fresh vegetables. It was a cost-effective side dish to include on the menu. Adding shredded cheese, turkey, bacon, and slices of hard-boiled egg made the salad into a satisfying alternative to a hot meal. A choice of dressings allowed diners to customize their salad.

Epic

The house dressing at Len Berg's was called Epic, and customers sometimes referred to it as French dressing. Unlike the commercially-bottled French dressing, Len Berg's version was clearly an oil-and-vinegar-based mix. The following recipe makes one quart.

DIRECTIONS

In a large bowl or unbreakable jar, combine 2 cups ketchup with 1 ½ cups Wesson oil, ½ cup apple cider vinegar, ⅓ cup sugar, 2 teaspoons pepper, 2 teaspoons salt, and 4 teaspoons paprika. Whisk or blend the ingredients until well mixed. Store in the refrigerator.

Blue Cheese

Blue Cheese Dressing was another Len Berg's favorite. Waitresses knew first-time customers by their reaction when the salad with a bright orange dressing arrived at the table: "But, I ordered blue cheese!" Service staff assured the customer the order was correct and took care not to identify it as "Roquefort dressing." (The Roquefort Association held restaurant owners responsible for false statements made about blue cheese dressing if it did not contain a defined percentage of Roquefort cheese.)

DIRECTIONS

Len Berg's blue cheese dressing was made by mixing 2 ½ pounds of blue cheese into 1 gallon of the house dressing (Epic) and 1 gallon mayonnaise.

Thousand Island

Many customers preferred a creamier salad dressing like Thousand Island Dressing.

DIRECTIONS

The following ingredients will yield 2 quarts: 4 hard-boiled eggs, chopped; 1 cup sweet pickle, chopped; 1 cup stuffed olives, chopped; 4 cups mayonnaise; and 4 cups ketchup. Combine the ingredients and mix until well-blended. Store in the refrigerator.

SALAD DRESSINGS

INGREDIENTS

Blue Cheese dressing:

2 ½ lbs. blue cheese

1 G. Epic dressing

1 G. mayonnaise

Thousand Island dressing:

4 hard-boiled eggs

1 C. sweet pickles

1 C. stuffed olives

4 C. mayonnaise

4 C. ketchup

Macaroon Pie

MACAROON PIE

INGREDIENTS

12 saltine crackers

1 C. sugar

1 tsp. baking powder

½ C. pecans

12 to 15 dates

3 egg whites

1 tsp. almond flavoring

whipped cream

One of the most popular desserts ever served at Len Berg's was macaroon pie. It was crunchy and rich and topped with soft whipped cream. When Len Berg's Restaurant catered events, Jeff Amerson sometimes had his staff create a dessert that was easier to serve than slices of pie. Instead of baking the ingredients in a pie pan, the cook dropped spoonfuls on a greased baking sheet to make "Macaroon Drops."

Regular diners knew that Len Berg's macaroon pie had no coconut, but cooks were often surprised to learn that saltine crackers were a primary ingredient. The local newspaper often printed the recipe in response to requests, and several home-grown community cookbooks included the recipe as well. Jeff Amerson always tried to remind publishers who sought the recipe that his version made three 9-inch pies. The 1957 issue of Duncan Hines' Adventures in Good Cooking included a version of the recipe for one pie.

DIRECTIONS

Roll 12 saltine crackers into fine crumbs and mix with 1 cup of sugar and 1 teaspoon baking powder. Chop ½ cup pecans and 12-15 dates, then add to the dry mix. Beat 3 egg whites until stiff. Add 1 teaspoon almond flavoring, then fold into the date, nut, and cracker mixture. Pour into a greased 9-inch pie pan or drop onto a greased or parchment-lined baking sheet. Bake pies for 30 minutes at 350 degrees. Serve with whipped cream.

Yield: One pie or about 2 dozen macaroon drops.

Logo designed for advertising in *The Macon Telegraph* and used on shirts and hats worn by staff. (c. 1986)

Jefferson D. Amerson, Sr. featured in an article in *Georgia Trend* magazine, May 1986.

A Second Helping

The Amerson Era: 1969-2003

The Barrys chose Jefferson Davis Amerson to carry on the legacy of Len Berg's.

Amerson and Art Barry first met when the theater manager from Macon hunted on the Amerson family farm in Washington County, Georgia. The summer before he graduated high school, Jeff Amerson came to Macon to live and work with his brother J.C. at Guy White's Radio Service, and Barry gave him a second job as an usher with Lucas & Jenkins Theatres. After high school, Amerson returned to Macon in 1943, planning to attend Navy V-12 School at Mercer. Once again, Barry gave him a job, this time at his new enterprise—Len Berg's Restaurant.

During his earliest months in Macon, Amerson went on an errand to Kress's Department Store, where he met a young woman decorating the Cherry Street store window. Later, when she worked at Davison's (formerly, Union) Department Store, Amerson was delighted to have Celia Drinnon step out the back door of her building and cross the alley to have lunch at Len Berg's. They courted in the days before H.M.F.P.I.C., so Amerson and Drinnon often strolled to Chapman's Pharmacy on the corner of Second and Mulberry to enjoy an ice cream cone before he returned to work the evening shift at the restaurant. The couple married in 1944, just before he entered the Army in 1945.

After basic training and preparing to serve his country, Amerson was ready to ship out from Staten Island, New York, when the war ended in Europe. Instead of venturing overseas, he was discharged from the Army in 1946, returned to Macon, and worked at Guy White Radio Service. Amerson also worked for a while at First National Bank before Barry recruited him to work at the restaurant. It was the final step toward a lifelong career. (In an interview from 1980, Amerson explained to a reporter, "This is the only job I've had for any length of time.")

Amerson's first jobs in the restaurant took him behind the scenes. He worked as a busboy and a dishwasher before Barry promoted him through the ranks, but it was the owner's way of teaching his young protégé all aspects of the business. Amerson quickly became an assistant manager and night manager. Then, in 1954, Jeff Amerson replaced Harold Norris as general manager of Len Berg's Restaurant.

When he and Celia first married, Jeff purchased a small farm in south Macon. In 1960, Texas and Art Barry helped them settle into a new home closer to Celia's family and Jeff's work. The Barrys realized the amount of time Jeff spent at the restaurant and the demands of raising three small children, so, as Celia recalled, "They did a lot for us when we were just starting out." The couples grew quite close, and when Celia was expecting her first child in 1948, the Barrys' daughter Patsy asked if she would name the baby after her.

Patsy Barry may have been disappointed when the Amersons had a boy, but Jeff was delighted to name his firstborn Jeff junior. The couple had two more sons—Steven, who died shortly after birth in 1950 and Jerry, who was born in 1954. Finally, when she had a baby girl in 1956, Celia honored Patsy's request and named the baby Patricia Ann.

Buster Barry, who was ten years old when Amerson started work at Len Berg's, grew up shadowing the young man as if he were an older brother. In later years, Buster described his relationship with Jeff Amerson as a "mutual admiration society of two" and seemed to understand his father's decision to support Amerson in acquiring the restaurant.

Amerson took majority interest in Len Berg's restaurant, and financial backer, Wallace M. Rivers was the secondary stockholder. Barry retained shares and maintained a small percentage for several key employees: Wilbur Mitcham, Pearl Mathis, Mary D. Cornelius, George Wilcher, and Thelma Woodard.

The 1969 sale came at a time when the restaurant industry was evolving yet again, but Amerson had learned valuable lessons from Barry and carried those forward as he took over: keep customers happy; keep traditional favorites and offer new items on the menu; and always, always, watch the bottom line. The new owner aimed to maintain the quality reflected in the restaurant's letterhead which he inherited with the purchase. It said, "Famous for Fine Food since 1908. Approved by the American Automobile Association, Recommended by Duncan Hines, Listed in *Gourmet's Guide to Good Eating* and *Dartnell's Favorite Restaurants*."

Amerson and Rivers made no major changes, and they kept veteran staff to deliver the courteous service that had always been a trademark of Len Berg's Restaurant. Some of the veteran staff started at Len Berg's about the same time as Amerson, and according to a 1985 article in *Restaurant News*, at least eleven employees had been working there since as early as 1950. George Wilcher started waiting tables at Len Berg's in 1944. Chef Wilbur Mitcham (who the article noted had "achieved near-legendary status in Macon") joined the restaurant in 1947.

Patrons continued to watch the staff dance through their daily routines, making everything about their service look easy. The customers knew the kitchen staff by their white uniforms and aprons. The waiters and busboys wore white jackets. And waitresses covered their white blouses with a smock or apron. Managers and hosts greeted guests in attire that reflected a business atmosphere, where they served businessmen, society matrons, tourists, and families, and the atmosphere was comfortable and welcoming, just as it had been when Barry owned the establishment.

Amerson made only small changes to the decor, adding a print of Jefferson Davis (president of the Confederacy) alongside the Kurz & Allison Civil War prints Barry had placed in the building. Amerson updated the group photo of the local board of realtors and hung it in the hallway near a shot of the

Macon Bar Association. Scenic landscapes of faraway places hung in one private dining room, and in another, images of Macon landmarks, including a photo of the Wesleyan Conservatory taken the day before Smitty (the part-time Len Berg's night host and full-time city firefighter) investigated the blaze that destroyed the historic structure. The new owner added golf memorabilia to one dining room and fishing paraphernalia in another to remind him of favorite pastimes.

Some Len Berg's waitresses decorated their tables with a small pot of citrus seedlings, a tradition started by Texas Barry. Celia Amerson added her touch as well. From her business, Evelyn Yates Flower Shop, the new owner's wife provided seasonal decorations, such as tiny Christmas trees for each table, wreaths for the doors, and a small skirted tree to take center stage on top of the cigarette vending machine in the front hall. The eclectic decor created a comfortable dining experience and provided entertainment for customers waiting for a table. Some studied the menu propped on the pay phone in the hall while others watched parting diners react to the sign next to the door: Press Button to Praise Cook. Patrons marveled at waitresses and busboys passing in the narrow hall without crashing into one another and dropping heavy plates or loaded bus-pans. It was like watching drivers on a busy California freeway swerve at just the right moment to avoid a mishap.

Macon's highways were not so crowded as those in LA, but the city had been a transportation hub for more than 150 years. River traffic had long ago given way to passenger trains by 1971, when the Nancy Hanks made its last run through the city, but Macon was now experiencing a new rush of traffic on Interstates 75 and 16. I-75 was a major north-south thoroughfare, taking automobiles from the northern border of the United States to sunny Florida. Many travelers stopped at the visitors' center north of Macon and found out about a little Southern-style restaurant a short distance off the highway. Drivers who spent three hours on their journey from Savannah to Macon were ready to stop for a meal, and many exited I-16 before it intersected with I-75 so they could cross the Ocmulgee River to find Len Berg's in the Post Office Alley.

Intersecting interstates allowed Macon to continue as a transportation center while it grew to be the hub of a different sort of movement in the 1970s. Capricorn Studio launched the careers of Southern rock musicians such as the Allman Brothers Band, Marshall Tucker Band, and Wet Willie. Among the businessmen who were daily customers, Len Berg's welcomed Capricorn

executives as well as members of the bands and their fans.

Southern rock bands often performed at the Macon Coliseum (later tagged the Centreplex), a multipurpose arena and convention center built in 1968, the year before Amerson and Rivers took ownership of Len Berg's. During the 1970s and 1980s, the Coliseum also hosted Elvis Presley (five shows), Led Zeppelin, Kenny Rogers, Bob Dylan, and others. The rodeo and high school basketball tournaments became annual events, and the Georgia Society of Square Dancers (of which, Jeff and Celia Amerson were members) brought thousands of participants to the city each fall. With each event, visitors who wanted to have a good meal before the show, found Len Berg's.

Amerson was delighted to see all types of events at the Coliseum, which was less than two miles from the Post Office Alley. (It was located in an area Leonard Berg had known as Cutter's Green when he lived there in the early 1900s.) Concerts and conventions brought diners into the restaurant, and that always helped the bottom line.

Independent restaurants nationwide grew to depend more and more on such events and tourism as a shift occurred in retail operations that affected downtown areas large and small. Macon's Westgate Shopping

Center had opened in 1961 as the first fully enclosed mall in Georgia. The shopping center had little negative impact on Macon's central business district because it did not lure large department stores from their downtown sites. Over the next fourteen years, though, the concept changed. When Macon Mall opened in 1975, it became the largest enclosed mall in the state, and it had a devastating affect on downtown. Sears left Walnut Street and Davison's left Cherry Street to join Belks and J.C. Penney's as anchor stores in the new mall. Smaller retailers, such as Joseph N. Neels and the Macon Shoe Company, stayed in place, but the majority of shoppers—and a lot of restaurant patrons—followed the large stores to the mall several miles west of the city's center.

Along with the shift in retail shopping, new franchise eateries came to Macon's suburbs. The city's independent restaurants, such as Len Berg's, Mark's Cellar, and the H & H, felt the effects, but rather than competing harder with one another, they often helped support each other. For instance, if the food supplier had closed for the weekend, one restaurant manager might call on his neighbor to borrow a critical ingredient. On a busy Friday night, the hostess at Mark's Cellar was happy to lend a few heads of lettuce or a case of chicken, knowing Len Berg's would be

ready to respond in kind, and they would repay the borrowed stock as soon as Mulberry Provision opened on Monday. She also counted on Amerson sending some Macaroon Pie as a tip.

As in Macon's earliest years, when wholesale grocers populated the downtown streets, food distributors such as Mulberry Provision positioned themselves near the railroad and in the business district. At one time, the company was directly across Wall Street Alley from Len Berg's, and the restaurant relied on fresh produce from the Farmers Market, too.

The Farmers Market replaced the City Market on the Green, which was located on Poplar Street in the 1800s. Both markets provided a venue for local farmers to sell produce to Macon shoppers and restaurant owners. The Farmers Market, established in the 1930s, was located near Poplar at the site of the old Findlay's Foundry on Oglethorpe Street. Amerson noted in an interview that when it was downtown, he shopped the Farmers Market daily for fresh vegetables for his restaurant.

That changed in 1976 when the Farmers Market followed the Macon Mall to the western outskirts of the city. Local produce companies and regional suppliers took over the role of supplying fresh produce, but if the delivery was late or the kitchen ran out of something, Amerson rushed staff to a grocery store to purchase emergency supplies. Like his independent colleagues, Amerson called on other restaurants downtown for help, but those were dwindling.

Community leaders, concerned about the viability of downtown Macon, searched for ways to keep the city alive and bustling. In 1982, the Keep Macon and Bibb County Beautiful campaign introduced the Cherry Blossom Festival, soon recognized as one of the South's top festivals. Macon welcomed busloads of tourists who came to see the springtime beauty of thousands of Yoshino cherry trees in bloom. Many visitors drifting through Third Street Park found their way to the alley and dined at Len Berg's for their first time. Locals who had a new reason to be downtown for festival activities brought out-of-town guests to a favorite spot for lunch. Festival-goers often turned their cameras over to Jerry Amerson (who joined the restaurant full time in 1979) to snap a photo of them all together before they strolled over to activities planned for the festival.

The influx of Cherry Blossom visitors brought interesting challenges for Len Berg's. For one thing, festival crowds often doubled the restaurant's business, and regular customers found a longer wait for a spot at the counter or their favorite booth. Though he appreciated the end result of the extra crowds, Jeff Amerson found he was not able to give customers as much personal time as he liked. Amerson didn't bump chair legs to rush customers along, as original owner Leonard Berg had been known to do, but he did try to speak to everyone who came through the restaurant's doors. He noted in a 1980 interview, "We're small enough we can do that. Besides, that's just part of the atmosphere people have come to expect." (Cecil Bently, 9/1/1980, *Macon Telegraph* "He adds down-home touch to downtown dining").

The final weekend of the Cherry Blossom Festival presented another challenge during its annual arts-and-crafts venue and street party. The parking lot at the restaurant was convenient to the Mulberry Street site of the showcase of artisans and the Cherry Street festivities on Saturday night. The Amersons found they had to monitor the lot and remind drivers that parking was reserved for Len Berg's customers. Many understood and stopped in for a meal before going on to the event, or they parked elsewhere.

Parking was an issue, too, when court was in session at the Federal Courthouse across the alley from Len Berg's. Once parking along Third Street or Mulberry filled to capacity, early morning court visitors found the vacant

Len Berg's Restaurant (1971). Photo courtesy of Middle Georgia Archives, Washington Memorial Library, Macon, Georgia.

parking lot behind the marble building tempting—at least until Amerson and his staff explained the lot was reserved for Len Berg's customers. Some promised to dine with them at lunchtime or at the end of the day, and Amerson walked the fine line of pleasing or upsetting a potential customer who had business in the courthouse.

Pleasing customers was what Amerson's business was all about, and he had plenty of practice with balancing their wants and needs. As public opinion about smoking in

crowds began to change, the restaurateur had to practice a new balancing act. As more and more customers complained about dining in a smoke-filled space, restaurants across the country looked for ways to accommodate both the smokers and nonsmokers. Amerson first designated one section of the building for smokers and put the nonsmokers on the other side of the restaurant. Customers who enjoyed a cigarette at the end of their meal grumbled a bit but soon adjusted. The wait staff soon observed, though, that tables in the nonsmoking area cleared quicker and provided them more opportunities to earn tips, so eventually, Amerson eliminated all smoking areas in the restaurant.

Years before clearing the air, Amerson had actually made room in his restaurant for a cigarette vending machine. A tobacco company sales representative convinced him it was an asset and kept the machine filled with popular cigarette brands. When he refilled the slots and emptied the change each week, the salesman left a portion of the proceeds with Amerson. Income from the machine was never enough, though, to balance out the problems it caused. The bulky box took up floor space across from the lunch counter, valuable space when customers were standing elbow to elbow waiting for a table. It also posed a temptation for thieves who broke into the restaurant in search of food and beer. They would pry open the box to swipe cigarettes and loose change—the only money left on the premises after the restaurant closed each day. Each time it happened, Amerson had to pay to repair and restock the machine. Finally, he tried adding a padlock to the vending machine to deter the thieves.

Another month, another break-in, and the padlock slowed the thieves only a bit. They dragged the machine outside so they had more room to work on smashing it open.

The next morning, after finding the broken vending machine in the parking lot, Amerson called the tobacco company and had them haul off the contraption for good.

With the cigarette machine gone, Amerson had one less worry, but break-ins continued. The possibility of free food and beer hidden away in an isolated location behind the post office continued to lure thieves. There was no cash left on the premises at night. Managers always left the register open, a visible cue so thieves would have one less thing to tear up, perhaps even eliminating their incentive altogether if they noticed the empty cash drawer before breaking a window.

To ensure there was no money in the building overnight, Len Berg's staff went to the bank several times each day. In the morning, they retrieved cash and coins to make change and after lunch and dinner, they delivered a deposit bag to the bank. In the 1970s, a manager carrying out the nightly deposit routine met with Len Berg's only incidence of serious crime. J.D. Smith (Smitty) was a city firefighter who moonlighted as a night manager at Len Berg's. One evening, as Smitty locked the doors of the empty restaurant and prepared to drive to the bank, two men approached and demanded the money he carried. Smitty did not comply. He tossed the deposit bag up onto the low roof of the restaurant and one of the men fired his weapon. A bullet grazed Smitty's arm, but he was spared a more serious injury when the men fled the scene.

After the robbery attempt, Amerson hired a security firm to escort the nightly deposit and drive through the alley at various intervals when the restaurant was closed. Having a uniformed officer on the premises late at night also eased the minds of customers as they walked to their cars in the dark parking lot.

Crime prevention had evolved since Leonard Berg's day, when a cot under the counter provided a place to rest when he or his brother stayed in the establishment overnight. The cot was long gone, replaced by coolers and equipment, but if a busboy was between places to stay, Amerson and his chef sometimes assigned a chore that kept the young man in the building overnight. Such a presence might have helped deter crime, but Amerson installed an even more effective electronic security system in the 1980s.

Amerson took the step, in part, to appease the insurance company. Electronic surveillance did not completely stop thieves, but it made an impact. On one occasion, while the senior Amerson was out of town, his son Jerry took a 2:00 AM call from the

security firm. They informed him the alarm was going off and that Macon police were in route to the restaurant to investigate a possible break-in. Jerry drove the deserted early morning streets to check on the situation.

When young Amerson arrived at the scene, he was pleased to learn police captured the intruder. The man, who was quite large in size, had tried to hide in the ladies' bathroom, where the only possible escape route was a tiny window into the back area of the kitchen. The police positioned officers in the kitchen and at the door into the bathroom, then warned if the man did not surrender, they would send Officer Bubba in to retrieve him. The thief was adamant he would not surrender until the police directed Officer Bubba—the eighty-pound Rottweiler —to speak.

Jeff and Jerry Amerson knew deserted city streets were a factor in the break-ins they experienced. As the city cycled through still another period of trying to lure people into downtown, some customers worried about driving into the area after dark. Downtown workers left for their homes in the suburbs when the courthouse and law firm across the alley closed around five o'clock. Macon Blueprint and other nearby offices and businesses shuttered their doors in the early evening as well. The nearby S&S Cafeteria on

Walnut Street left its location around the corner to move closer to residences further north on Riverside Drive. The Town Pavilion motel, which opened to popular acclaim in the 1960s, was declining, and Len Berg's customers felt uneasy about its latest residents. Amerson recognized what Barry had explained years ago—there was a certain charm to having the restaurant tucked into an alley—but he considered whether it might be time for a change.

At one point during this consideration, Amerson and his partner, Wallace Rivers, purchased a parcel of land on the corner of Walnut and Third Streets. It had been the site of the Bell House Restaurant, and they considered moving Len Berg's to the more visible location. Remembering the impact on business when the restaurant had relocated to the Terminal Station during Barry's ownership, Amerson proceeded carefully. In the end, the men chose not to leave the alley.

Some customers suggested that instead of abandoning their alley location, Len Berg's should open additional restaurants in locations such as near their home in Milledgeville or Forsyth or Perry. Customers proposed a branch of Len Berg's on the Georgia coast, perhaps at St. Simons Island. Eventually, late in the 1970s, Amerson and Rivers obliged by opening The Seafood

Restaurant in the former Pinebrook Inn on Forsyth Road.

Mickey Rivers, son of Amerson's business partner, managed the new venture. A familiar red dinner menu announced the restaurant was "under direction of Len Berg's" and featured the same hand-cut steaks, seafood, and desserts diners found downtown at Len Berg's in the alley. Mickey Rivers had worked with Amerson as an assistant manager and night manager at Len Berg's, so he understood the restaurant's policies and practices. Still, the owners found The Seafood Restaurant could not replicate the success of its parent, and always aware of the bottom line, Amerson decided the costs required to operate a second full-service restaurant were not worth it. It was time to try something else.

Amerson moved to another concept, one he was familiar with because of his mentor, Art Barry. In the mid-1960s, Barry had opened a carryout restaurant, and his son, Buster, went on to have great success with the independent Pick-Up Meals by Barry. Amerson began to promote carryout service from his own restaurant in the alley while he searched for a location to replicate the early Meals to Go by Len Berg's.

In 1979, Amerson opened Len Berg's Carryout on Hemlock Street, just across from the Medical Center of Central Georgia. For lunch or dinner, medical staff and hospital visitors walked the short distance to a small building across the street. They placed their order, much as one would at a fast-food chain, but instead of the usual fare of greasy hamburgers and fries, a tasty array of meats and vegetables made up the menu. Customers savored the home-style cooking prepared by cooks who had worked at Len Berg's in the alley before moving to the Hemlock location.

Whether they heard local radio personality Bill Powell read the menu on his daily morning show or referred to the board posted behind the counter, customers found a food selection that changed each day. They marked their choices on an individual slip of paper, added their name, and watched as the cashier passed their order to the kitchen. Within a few minutes, the customer had a steaming hot meal dished into a Styrofoam container to keep it warm. There were no waiters or waitresses, no cloth napkins or heavy china plates, but customers could find a few tables if they decided to dine in. Most hurried back to the hospital with their order, some carrying flowers they bought next door at Evelyn Yates Florist. It was a secondary location of the business owned and operated by Celia Amerson and her daughter, Patsy.

Amerson knew from his days with Art Barry how important it was to keep his business moving forward. In 1982, not long after opening the new carryout, Amerson decided the daily crowds downtown warranted an expansion of the existing building. The addition on one end of the restaurant accomplished a vision created a half-century earlier. In the original plans, Berg and architect Ella Ellis League designed two large rooms that could be divided into smaller dining areas or left open to accommodate large parties. The new wing added thirty seats to the restaurant's capacity, allowing them to seat as many as one hundred patrons at a time.

Len Berg's hosts guided patrons through Room 6 into the new space, a large, open room which allowed for parties of more than ten people to be seated together. The addition also included an office that provided additional customer seating, an interior entrance to the walk-in cooler, and a pantry. The windows in Rooms 4 and 5 offered a peek through into the new space which was decorated with familiar Kurz & Allison prints and cast-iron cookware from the front areas of the restaurant.

Construction of the new addition matched the original building so well customers hardly noticed. Even before then, Len Berg's owners often fielded questions about the

Chefs Leon Blash and Wilbur Mitcham serving H.M.F.P.I.C. at the ribbon-cutting for an addition to the building. The addition was named the Arthur P. Barry Dining Room (June 1982)

origins of their building since it was so unlike the noisy, open dining rooms in many casual restaurants. Not realizing the structure was designed to be a restaurant, some people thought it must have been an old stable or perhaps, since it was so close to the courthouse, it had been a jail in its past life. The Amersons explained the restaurant had been built there in 1950. To the persistent customers who wanted to know, "Yes, but what was here before?" they smiled and offered, "Well, before Len Berg's, it was the Smith's back yard."

The 1982 expansion opened with a ribbon-cutting celebration that featured H.M.F.P.I.C. dished up by chefs Wilbur Mitcham and Leon Blash. Mrs. Texas Barry did the honors, surrounded by Celia Amerson, Buster and Carolyn Barry. (Art Barry had died in December, 1980.) Special guests at the grand opening included family friend Kenneth Taylor as well as Betty Cartwright, who worked many years as a bookkeeper for the restaurant. E.H. Holloway, who had also worked at Len Berg's, was another special guest. Holloway was a retired railroad man who greeted guests at lunchtime and "ran the tickets" to compile data about each day's sales. Years later, Jerry Amerson recalled how Mr. Holloway would stand in the parking lot during a break, holding his railroad watch and listening to trains as they passed several blocks away.

Retired railroad man E.H. Holloway runs the tickets after lunch.

A Second Helping

The expansion was good for the brisk lunch business in the alley. The carryout location on Hemlock Street added to the daily success of Len Berg's, but after only a few years, Amerson learned of building plans at the Medical Center that would force him to close his business there. A developer approached him about opening a carryout in a strip of offices and small retail shops he was building on Northside Drive, so Amerson and his son made plans for the new carryout operation. The interior of the small space was filled with a few booths for eat-in dining, a counter for placing orders, and limited kitchen space in the back: steam table, fry pot, and a small cooler. They returned to the original model Barry had used, in which most of the food was prepared downtown so it could be transported to the carryout. The Amersons ordered multi-colored cathedral glass for windows on either side of the door to provide customers with a visible reminder of the parent Len Berg's. On May 3, 1984, family friend Kenneth Taylor purchased the first order at the new Carryout, just as he had done when Amerson opened the Hemlock diner. Taylor paid $3.80 for a meal of turkey & dressing, turnip greens, buttered carrots, salad, and tea.

Three years later, the Amersons purchased a building on the corner of Ingleside and Rogers avenues in the area known as Ingleside Village. The structure had been a gas service station and was an anchor to Ingleside Village, a development of retail shops and professional offices sitting in the midst of a residential district. Ingleside Avenue was several blocks over from Vineville Avenue, a major thoroughfare in Macon, and it was convenient to people on their way home from work. Jeff and Jerry Amerson hired a local contractor, Reginald Broxton, to renovate the station and transform it from a fuel stop to a food stop.

The newest Len Berg's Carryout used the service bay and interior of the gas station for the kitchen and prep area. Steam tables, work tables, an ice machine and tea containers now filled the space where the station owners had once stocked automotive supplies, soft drinks and snacks. The large open service bays were reconstructed to provide space in the large kitchen for ovens, grills, fry pots, a walk-in cooler, and ample counter space for Irene to mix and assemble pies. Irene baked seventeen pies each morning, enough for Len Berg's Restaurant downtown and for the carryout: four meringue (lemon or chocolate) as well as four apple and nine macaroon pies. Moving the pie-baking functions to the carryout relieved the cramped conditions in the kitchen downtown, and the basement of the new site provided ample storage for catering supplies.

To accommodate customers who wanted to dine in, without the frills of a full restaurant, space was added to the front of the reconstructed building. A large open room was built between the original storefront and where gas pumps had been. Six booths lined the half brick and half glass walls between the front door and the counter where patrons placed their order. Again, the Amersons instructed the builder to flank the front door with familiar multicolored windows.

The modern front door at the Carryout was glass, not at all like the heavy wooden doors at the alley downtown. The booths were modern, too. Carryout customers quickly learned the atmosphere and service were different, and that was okay. The Ingleside and Northside patrons focused on "fast food" they could take home, and for those who chose to eat in, plastic utensils wrapped in a paper napkin was part of the deal. Instead of interacting with waiters or waitresses, the regulars greeted a cashier or spoke to an apron-clad cook who dipped their food into a Styrofoam container. If they wanted Coca-cola, they knew not to expect the small glass bottles used at Len Berg's downtown, but some of the regulars knew where to find the tea dispenser on their own if they needed a

Jerry Amerson at Len Berg's Ingleside Avenue carryout location. (1988)

refill and the staff was tied up with a line of customers.

The convenience of Len Berg's Carryout seemed to begin outweighing the atmosphere of dining downtown in the evening. Patrons appreciated being able to stop on their way home to order a meal they could eat in the comfort of their home, in slippers and comfortable clothes. They also knew that except for the steaks and seafoods offered only at dinner, they could expect the same good food they would find at the parent restaurant. The Northside and Ingleside Avenue locations reached a volume of dinner sales that matched Len Berg's main restaurant.

A Second Helping

Cook Lorenzo Lamar in the kitchen at Len Berg's (1975).

Cooks at the Ingleside carryout, including employees like Irene and Leon and Rosetta, used the same recipes they had learned from Annette or Chef (Wilbur Mitcham) or Mary Dee. They continued Len Berg's tradition of good food, but over time, customers began to note a subtle difference in the flavor of foods served in the separate locations. (For example, some preferred their holiday turkey and dressing from the Ingleside carryout because it had more cornbread flavor than the Thanksgiving or Christmas orders that came from downtown.) Amerson understood the main concern was that customers were happy with their food, but if he received complaints or noted more than a subtle difference, the owner reminded his cooks to adjust their recipes. He explained that one key to Len Berg's long-term success was staying constant: "People know the same people are preparing and serving the food, so they know what to expect when they come in." With cooks like Mary Dee, Pearl, Thelma, Lorenzo "Judge Lo," Leon, Rosetta, Annette or Irene, his customers had a long track of high expectations.

Managing recipe consistency was easiest downtown where Chef Wilbur Mitcham kept a close eye on food preparations and made sure everyone stayed true to the recipes, whether they were written down or not. Most of the cooks had been with Len Berg's for years and simply cooked by rote memory. Any one of them could fill in at another's work station, but some had their particular speciality. For instance, Annette Washington was, according to Buster Barry, "the best baker in Macon, if not in the entire state. She would get mighty upset if the rolls didn't turn out right." Then Barry added, "Everyone cared about the food they prepared."

Those caring cooks were the first to arrive at Len Berg's each morning, before the managers and waitresses. They moved from the walk-in cooler or pantry to the kitchen; they sliced and diced, mixed and kneaded; they stood on their feet over a hot stove or fry pot, oven or steam table, taking short breaks to sit in the back hall only when the rush was over. On a typical day, the cooks prepared twenty quarts of peas, thirty quarts of butterbeans, 100 pounds of potatoes, fifty pounds of snap beans, four pork loins, twenty-five to thirty chickens, a case of salmon, forty pounds of trout, twenty pounds of ground beef, 200 ears of corn, and enough dessert to satisfy the hundreds of customers Len Berg's would see that day.

While cooks prepared the food, busboys shuttled supplies to and from the kitchen, made twenty gallons of iced tea and almost as much Savarin coffee. They swept the floors to be sure they were clean for the 11:00 AM opening, even though they knew they would sweep again at the end of the shift. Sometimes Amerson sent a busboy on a last-minute run over to Mulberry Provision to pick up supplies, and Willie made the mail run to Ingleside to retrieve Irene's pies. Waiters and waitresses arrived just before 11:00, in time to fill sugar containers, fold napkins, wipe down ketchup bottles, and set tables.

Hostess Mae Layson. (1994)

The kitchen staff represented decades of service to Len Berg's, but so did the staff who directly served the customers. Waiter George Wilcher started at the restaurant in 1944, during the Barry era, and he retired in the 1980s. Loyal customers often deferred being seated until George had a table open. It was the same for others such as Tommy Watson, Miss Ruby or Miss Mae, Jean, Brenda, or Kerry. Customers counted on their favorite waiter or waitress to know their beverage preference or whether they wanted their corn dished up in the divided plate or in a small bowl so it didn't run over into the turnips.

With their friendly efficiency, the waiters, waitresses, and busboys helped give the impression that providing customer service was easy. Sometimes, customers suggested to Amerson that he had a perfect job: "All you have to do is be pleasant and find a seat for people." The owner did not argue the point, but he knew the customer who offered the comment did not see the hours of his day that went into keeping books, placing orders, juggling schedules, maintaining the building, and the myriad details required to keep a successful restaurant running.

Amerson's "perfect" job was full-time, taking more than 300 days each year. Some Macon restaurants closed for a week so their entire staff could vacation at once, but Len Berg's stayed open Monday through Saturday, fifty-two weeks a year. They closed on Sundays and four holidays: Fourth of July, Labor Day, Thanksgiving Day, and Christmas Day. To ensure his customers were not surprised by a holiday closing, Amerson usually reminded them with a sign on the front door and an ad in the newspaper. The Labor Day advertisement often claimed "Gone Fishing," and when Jerry Amerson took over the

Lunch crowd at Len Berg's. (1983)

restaurant in 1993, it changed to "Gone Birding."

Len Berg's staff took vacations, just not all at once. The manager shuffled work schedules so individuals could take time off without disrupting the kitchen or service routines. Jeff and Jerry Amerson took their vacations in spurts—a long weekend for the Georgia-Florida football game or a birding trip to Arizona. They often left the restaurant in the hands of their capable assistant manager Jake Clarke, or Rudy Gray on Saturday, and sometimes, both Amersons found themselves at Lake Sinclair for the weekend. Their Saturday night routine included a phone call to Jake or Rudy at closing time, just to check in.

On occasion, Jerry went birding on the Georgia coast or made an overnight visit with his in-laws near Dublin. Trusted staff and his father took care of things at the restaurant, but still, as he drove back home on Sunday afternoon, Jerry barely had to steer his truck off the interstate ramp and through the quiet downtown streets to Len Berg's in the alley. He looked around the lot as he parked parallel to the building and made sure things were in order. Then he walked through the restaurant listening to the familiar sounds—the time clock, the cooler motor, the echoes of an empty kitchen. When Buster Barry and Jerry compared notes years after both had left the business, each recalled a similar Sunday afternoon routine. Jerry listened to the heartbeat of the building. Buster noticed the smells: "I could walk in the front door and tell if something in the cooler had gone bad."

The Sunday afternoon or holiday check on Len Berg's was a lifetime habit for the Amersons. Both Jerry and his father spent time at each location of their business almost every day. They did not attend meetings of the Rotary Club, Exchange Club, or other civic groups that met at noon. Though he supported the idea of these organizations, Jeff Amerson felt it did not serve his business well for the owner to be absent during the busiest time of the day.

On one rare occasion (a Tuesday in 1991), both Amersons left the restaurant just before noon. They left the lunch duties to assistant manager Jake Clarke while they drove three miles to the Ocmulgee National Monument. Father and son climbed the steps to the top of the Great Temple Mound to watch the moon cover the sun in a once-in-a-lifetime solar eclipse. The astrological event was brief, and the Amersons soon returned to their routine—Jerry to work at the restaurant and Jeff to a game of golf.

Jeff Amerson had begun to leave more and more of the management duties to his capable son, realizing that at least one Amerson would be present during the lunch rush. The senior Amerson played more golf, spent more time fishing with Celia or friends, and learned to enjoy leisure time. He did not, though, walk away from Len Berg's altogether.

Often, Jeff played a round of golf early in the day or after the lunch rush so he could be in the restaurant at mid-day to greet customers and maintain a presence. He might slap a friend on the shoulder and laugh about a joke, or he would check on the party of ladies in Room 3 to ask if everything was "good." (He avoided asking if everything was fine because he felt that was not a sufficient endorsement of the food and service at his restaurant.) At the end of the day, no matter where he was, the senior Amerson called Jerry to find out how business had been.

Jerry Amerson settled into the responsibilities of managing the restaurant with full knowledge of its demands. To ease the burden of managing three locations of the restaurant, he and his father decided to let the lease on the Northside carryout property expire and reduce the business to two locations.

Jerry and his father knew staff could certainly handle minor emergencies, but they also understood that liability issues and insurance claims always fell on the owners' shoulders. The assistant manager and other Len Berg's staff knew what to do if a customer tripped over a purse on the floor or if someone burned their hand in the kitchen. (Although Jerry occasionally had to remind kitchen staff to ignore the old wives' tale of putting grease on a burn, most of the time the veterans knew to apply ice to cool it). The proprietor had to give final word or make the call if the air conditioner broke just before opening on a Saturday morning in August or if the plumbing in the ladies room backed up during the dinner rush on a Friday night. After all, the owners were responsible for the bill to bring in plumbers and others on overtime.

Assistant Manager Jake Clarke (c. 1991)

Preventive maintenance helped keep the equipment and facility functioning properly, but as the building constructed in 1950 began to age, problems were bound to crop up. Chef Mitcham took care of minor repairs, things like greasing a door hinge, touching up paint in the hallway, or using a special wrench to tighten brackets that held the stools upright at the lunch counter.

Having lunch at the counter at Len Berg's. (1971)

Larger jobs required professional help, and the Amersons tried to schedule contractors to work at night or on Sunday so they would not disrupt service.

Occasionally, though, service was disrupted. When repairs forced a shut-down, staff took vacation time, or if possible, they worked at the carryout. Chef kept the busboys on the payroll by scheduling extra heavy-duty cleaning chores in the kitchen or areas where they wouldn't be in the way of contract repairmen.

During one occasion when Len Berg's closed for emergency repairs, Jerry Amerson observed the single-mindedness of a hungry customer.

A major water/sewer line in the men's room clogged, and Jerry called for help. The plumbers moved all the fixtures out of the tiny space so they had room to work, and since the restaurant was closed for business, Chef directed his crew to move heavy equipment to the front hall so they could scrub down the greasy kitchen walls. He directed the busboys to clean the carpet outside the men's room and remove it to the parking lot to dry and so it was out of the way for the plumbers. At noon, a woman startled Jerry when she squeezed past a refrigerator and stepped up to the counter to ask what time the restaurant would be opening for the day. He shook his head about the story in later years: This woman had parked next to a plumber's truck—almost the only vehicle in the lot at noon—walked on a piece of wet carpet and past a toilet sitting outside by the front door, stepped over pipes and squeezed by heavy kitchen equipment, but somehow seemed shocked that Len Berg's was closed for the day!

The restaurant was closed for repairs again a few years later after a car crashed through the front of the building. It happened on a Saturday morning, just before the restaurant opened for lunch. A customer parking her car near the front door stepped on the accelerator instead of the brake. Chef had been sitting at the counter, but since it was almost time for their first regular to arrive, he vacated the seat that customer preferred. The waitress set a menu, napkin, and utensils in the spot before following Chef into the kitchen as he went to check on final preparations for dinner.

Fortunately, the customer was late arriving. Busboys and the other waitresses were in rooms down the hall or in the kitchen, folding napkins fresh from the laundry, filling salt shakers, and setting tables. When they heard the crash, everyone rushed to the front and found a rainbow of glass shards littering the floor in front of the bumper of a Mercedes peeking through the brick wall.

Jerry Amerson, who was working the Saturday shift, checked on the driver and tried to calm her. Then he called the company from whom he leased the building so they could assess the damage and call the insurance company: no injuries, but the restaurant had to be closed until repairs could be made.

Amerson made the calls, and following an initial inspection, the contractor's crew boarded up the gaping hole. That secured the building until the contractor could gather supplies and begin work. By Tuesday morning, the men had finished their work, and the only sign of the incident was the smell of fresh paint. The downtown location of Len Berg's was back in business after only a brief disruption.

A few years later, businesses throughout Macon were disrupted for several weeks for a different reason altogether, and Len Berg's felt the effects of the disaster as well. In July 1994 Tropical Storm Alberto brought heavy rains to central Georgia. The Ocmulgee River rose to record heights, flooding streets and interstate interchanges, and stranding motorists. The greatest challenge Alberto brought to the city came when flood waters breached Macon's water treatment facility. The city's water was contaminated and declared undrinkable until repairs were made to the facility.

Restaurants throughout Macon scrambled to find a way to operate during the three weeks before the city's water treatment plant returned to normal operations. Len Berg's carryouts had a long tradition of using disposable plates and utensils, so they had a good quantity on hand. Jerry Amerson moved some of the inventory to the alley as he waited for suppliers to catch up on delivering the hot item to restaurants all over the city. Friends, employees, and family banded together to help Amerson. His wife's father and brother secured a new water tank from a neighboring farm in Emanuel County and brought it to Macon. They installed plumbing on the tank to run potable water into the building for the cooks to use as they prepared meals or washed pots and pans. Jerry's sister, Patsy, and her husband hitched the tank to a trailer each evening and drove to Jones County to refill with fresh water to

Waitress Nita Ware. (1991)

Waitress Jan Wilson (c. 1998)

deliver to the carryout and downtown restaurant. Len Berg's survived the Great Flood of 1994 with only minimal disruption.

As if operating a restaurant on a daily basis wasn't challenging enough, backed-up sewer lines, car crashes, and a mighty flood added to the task Jerry Amerson faced as he took over the restaurant from his father. In all its history—from 1908 until 1992—Len Berg's Restaurant had not seen a succession of ownership from father to son. Berg's boys went into medicine, architecture, and history. Barry's son branched out on his own and established a career in commercial real

estate. Even Jerry's older brother chose a different line of work. Jeff Amerson, Jr., did a stint at the restaurant during high school, bussing tables and cleaning up the kitchen, but then he joined the Marines and attended college before going to work in the medical field.

Jerry attended college, too, working part-time at the restaurant while he earned a degree in biology at Georgia College in Milledgeville. Young Amerson accepted his father's offer of a full-time position at Len Berg's in 1979, the same year he married and moved back to Macon. Over the next several

Jerry Amerson slowing down to have a bite to eat. (1995)

years, Jeff Amerson acquired remaining shares of Len Berg's stock, and he and Celia appointed Jerry as president and manager of the restaurant late in 1992.

It was easy for Len Berg's staff and customers to see a difference in the Amerson father and son. Jeff was gregarious and passionate about his role as a restaurateur, but although Jerry enjoyed interacting with employees and patrons, he was much more reserved. Jerry preferred a quiet walk in the woods to the camaraderie of a golf game, and he was more likely to encourage others to tell jokes where his father was often leading into at least one more funny story. Jerry learned from his father about managing a restaurant. He was like all his predecessors, who realized the strength of their business depended on loyal employees, and he was less fiery than his father when it came time to deal with personnel issues. The strength of loyal employees proved critical when Len Berg's Restaurant suffered a major loss.

A half-century after he first went to work at the Macon restaurant, Jefferson Davis Amerson died on February 16, 1993. Although he had turned the restaurant over to his son several months earlier, Jeff Amerson was still part of the heart and soul of Len Berg's.

Chef Wilbur Mitcham, another part of Len Berg's heart and soul, helped the younger Amerson through the grief of losing his father, business partner, and mentor. Chef understood when Jerry reached an especially difficult decision on a topic he and his father had discussed for the past year: it was time to close the restaurant in the evenings.

Jerry and Jeff Amerson had looked at all the issues. There were no theaters or retail shops open late enough to draw people to Cherry or Mulberry Streets, residences on Walnut Street had long ago been replaced by offices, and workers who crowded into the restaurant for lunch were ready to head home to families in the suburbs at the end of the day.

Though they might have been disappointed, faithful customers, who had also witnessed the decline in traffic on downtown streets at night, certainly understood. Some customers voiced their dismay about missing the restaurant's signature filet mignon or stuffed shrimp, items that were only on the dinner menu, but Jerry took their comments in stride. The words he had trouble swallowing came from infrequent patrons who, months later, would scold, "When did y'all decide to close at night? I always came down here for dinner, especially on Friday nights!"

Jerry would thank the person for their comment and for choosing to have lunch at Len Berg's. Then he privately observed that if those customers had been as regular about dining in the evenings as they claimed, perhaps the bottom line of sales would have warranted keeping the restaurant open at night.

Many customers missed the steaks that had long been a signature of Len Berg's Restaurant, so Jerry put filet mignon on the lunch menu downtown and added it to the menu at the carryout, too. He worked with a local supplier to meet the restaurant's high standard for the steak, but slow sales and cost control soon factored into the decision to take the filet mignon off the menu for good.

Jerry tried to maintain other traditions, especially in the wake of so many changes: He advertised the beginning of summer with the traditional H.M.F.P.I.C. announcement; he tweaked the Labor Day ad but gave his loyal employees a well-deserved break; he kept the restaurant open on New Year's Day so patrons could start their year off right with the traditional dish of black-eyed peas.

When the world came to Georgia for the International Olympic Games in 1996, many businesses saw it as an opportunity to display the tradition of Southern hospitality. Macon

Waiter Tommy Watson was a favorite of many loyal customers (1991).

was not a venue for any of the games, but the local Convention and Visitors Bureau made sure tourists knew the city was only an hour's drive south of Atlanta. As a result, Len Berg's welcomed a large number of world travelers in 1996. But the restaurant had always catered to travelers. Berg often served men and families traveling for business or pleasure. Barry introduced a favorite menu item in response to tourists searching for something peachy. And Jeff Amerson welcomed visitors who drifted into Macon for the annual Cherry Blossom Festival. Tourists who stayed at the 1842 Inn on

College Street heard about Len Berg's from the proprietors, and other visitors followed directions provided at the I-75 rest stop north of Macon. Some new customers explained they had read about Len Berg's in an old *Brown's Guide to Georgia* or in an issue of *Georgia Trend* magazine. Readers of *Southern Living* magazine agreed with the article "Southern Food Right" when it said about Len Berg's, "This is the kind of place where you compare everything on the menu to the way your mama made it." Jerry Amerson thanked them for the praise and clarified, "It's true—if your mama is from the South."

After all, Len Berg's cooks were Southern to the core. They knew soul food, and the man who led the kitchen had been at the business of restaurant cooking for a lifetime.

Chef Wilbur Mitcham started working at Len Berg's in 1947, seven years before Jerry Amerson was born. The young owner had never known the restaurant without Chef, and in an interview from 1998, Amerson's response to a reporter asking about Mitcham's influence on the business was, "It wouldn't seem right without him here."

Mitcham grew up in Macon and started his career in food service when he was just twelve years old. He worked at cafes, restaurants, and "greasy spoons" in the area —waiting tables, washing dishes, and learning to cook. He married Annie Mae Leonard in 1942 and served in the Army during World War II. After the war, Mitcham landed in New York City for a time, and it was there he worked for and learned from an Asian chef.

Chef and Ms. Annie raised their large family in Macon, instilling in them a love of education and a strong work ethic. Columnist Ed Grisamore wrote about Wilbur Mitcham in 1998, noting his long partnership with Ms. Annie and the family they raised. At least nine of their children earned college degrees, and one child made a career in the Air Force. The Mitchams influenced people outside of their immediate family, too. Ms. Annie worked in the Bibb County school system for almost forty years, and after she sent her own children to college, the family matriarch earned a degree in religious education from Wesleyan College.

Grisamore also wrote about Wilbur Mitcham's compassion for others, including how he went almost daily to take food and clothing to homeless people under the bridge at Spring Street. The Amersons and Barrys witnessed Chef's influence when he brought young boys to work as busboys at Len Berg's. It was often their first opportunity to earn money, and several stayed with the restaurant many years, some learning to be cooks under Chef's tutelage. Mitcham once explained, "I've taught a lot of other people how to cook. You've got to show a lot of love and not think you know it all."

Chef demonstrated his love for his work for more than fifty years at Len Berg's, and it involved much more than stirring the pot.

Mitcham arrived each morning by 6:00 AM to supervise the day's food preparation. After Ms. Annie retired from her work in the school system, he often left after a few hours, claiming it was time to go home and see what "Mother" had on her honey-do list for the day. He would hang up his apron and exchange the floppy white chef's hat for his old gray fedora. As he retrieved his keys, Chef bid farewell saying, "I'm gonna do something the devil won't—I'm gonna leave y'all alone for a while."

Later in the day, Mitcham returned to supervise busboys to make sure they did a good job cleaning up and that the kitchen was in good order for the next meal. When the restaurant was open for dinner, he spent his evening supervising the kitchen and cooking steaks for customers or a special serving of chop suey for Jerry and his wife.

Chef Wilbur Mitcham on his way home between lunch and dinner. (1991)

In late fall/early winter of 2002, Chef suffered a debilitating stroke. He died the following year on Father's Day, and the Mitcham family was not alone in feeling the loss. Macon's homeless lost a compassionate friend; young African-American boys lost a mentor; the community lost an icon; and Len Berg's Restaurant lost another part of its heart and soul.

Even before Chef's illness, Jerry Amerson had started a conversation with his wife and mother about a future when he was no longer at Len Berg's. Although not directly involved in restaurant operations, both women had lived with the business and knew the heavy responsibilities of operating a restaurant. They understood it required tremendous commitment and passion, forces that seemed to leave with Jeff Amerson and Wilbur Mitcham.

The Amersons agreed Len Berg's Restaurant should keep going. But they knew it was more than a family business, it was a Macon tradition. So they commissioned Charles Jay, a local commercial realtor, to help find new owners. A young couple who seemed ready to put their own hearts and souls into the venture made an offer, and in October 2003 Len Berg's opened its doors with new owners. Though the couple consulted with Jerry a few weeks after the sale, this represented the first time in more than fifty

years that Len Berg's operated without an Amerson on staff.

For a while, Amerson's manager, Rudy Gray, stayed on, as well as cooks, busboys, and servers who had worked at the restaurant for a long time. They provided the consistency Jeff Amerson had highlighted as being so important to a restaurant's success.

The new owners tried to make the transition to new ownership a success, and began to introduce minor changes to the menu, just as Berg, Barry, and the Amersons had done from time to time. They added new dishes and took others off the menu. Customers began to notice subtle differences in the flavor of familiar foods, which was not unlike the differences that had been detected between food at the separate locations of the restaurant.

But regular patrons began to complain when they noticed more of their favorite items missing from the menu, or when they missed veteran staff who left to find work elsewhere. Patrons who had once delighted in receiving their Coca Cola in the old-fashioned 6-ounce glass bottles were disappointed to find the new owners serving canned sodas. It seemed to be a minor difference, one that saved money for the owners, but the change suggested a disregard for traditional favorites. Still, new customers read about Len

Berg's and found their way to the iconic restaurant, and some loyal customers remained faithful about having lunch in the alley or grabbing their food to go at the carryout on Ingleside Avenue.

An unfortunate part of the transition came when the couple was hit with unexpected expenses. Because of the transfer in ownership, the new owners had to make expensive upgrades to the fifty-year-old kitchen downtown in order to receive a business license in their names. The unpleasant surprise added to the financial burdens the young couple already faced as they were striving to make their dream a reality, so less than two years after the Amersons sold Len Berg's, the restaurant closed.

The community missed their Len Berg's, and a few months later, a long-time Macon family contacted the bank to secure assets so they could reopen the establishment. But before the family could secure a lease on the downtown property, a neighboring business had taken over almost all of the parking spaces around the restaurant. Perhaps in Berg's day, pedestrians made up the bulk of his customers, but ninety years after he established the business, diners often preferred to drive to the restaurant. The newest owners decided to operate the restaurant at the site of the Len Berg's

Carryout on Ingleside Avenue and hoped to find a suitable downtown location to expand once they had reestablished the business.

Once again, in January 2006, Macon diners enjoyed familiar Len Berg's food. The new owners contacted Jerry Amerson and asked him to review favorite menus and help locate former employees who might want to work at the restaurant again. Seven employees who had worked with Amerson returned, each bringing twenty to thirty-seven years of Len Berg's experience with them. It was not enough.

Again, the new owners were required to make structural changes to the building in order to secure a business license. It set them back from their goal of opening a second location downtown, but they worked to build the business back to Len Berg's successful days. On November 1, 2007, however, the *Macon Telegraph* announced, "Once again, Len Berg's—a name synonymous with Southern-style food—has closed in Macon."

Today, Len Berg's remains closed. But, it also remains in the hearts and on the minds of people who worked or dined there during its long history. They still savor memories of warm bread or cold, sweet tea and recall the sights and sounds and aromas of a place that felt like home. They can still remember pressing a button to ring a bell to praise the cook or think of favorite foods they ordered by the letter. Some can still recount the 278 steps from their office to the front door of Len Berg's in the alley.

For many, even though the restaurant is no longer a place where they can put their feet under the table and enjoy a satisfying meal of signature good food, Len Berg's will always hold a place in memory as the place to find H.M.F.P.I.C. and other good food.

Celia Amerson and her son Jerry Amerson, July, 1993.

RECIPES FROM THE AMERSON ERA

Barbecued Short Ribs of Beef

Salmon Croquettes

Filet Mignon

Macaroni and Cheese

Fried Corn

Corn Sticks

Boston Cream Pie

Cherry Cobbler

Turkey and Dressing

Fried Oysters

Stuffed Shrimp

Carrot and Raisin Salad or Cole Slaw

Fried Apples

Southern Succotash

Vegetable Soup

Beets in Orange Sauce

Lemon Meringue Pie

A Second Helping

Barbecued Short Ribs of Beef

Jeff Amerson made a career of serving customers at Len Berg's. He followed Art Barry and Leonard Berg's practice of using the best cuts of meat, and one of his favorite dishes—to serve and to eat—was Barbecued Short Ribs of Beef.

DIRECTIONS

Preheat oven to 400 degrees.

RIBS:

Cut beef short ribs into portions of 1 pound each and place in a roasting pan; pour a half-and-half mixture of vinegar and water to a depth halfway up the portions of meat. Cover and bake for about 2 hours. Uncover and drain off most of the liquid. Reduce heat to 350 degrees and continue baking another hour or until nicely browned. Remove and serve with sauce.

BARBECUE SAUCE:

Combine ingredients in sauce pan and simmer for about one hour on top of the stove and pour over ribs when ready to serve.

BARBECUED SHORT RIBS OF BEEF

INGREDIENTS

10 lbs. beef short ribs

1 to 2 C. water

1 to 2 C. apple cider vinegar

Barbecue Sauce:

1 C. ketchup

1 C. apple cider vinegar (or a half-and-half mixture of vinegar and pickle juice)

3 Tbsp. Worcestershire sauce

1 Tbsp. Tabasco sauce

salt and pepper to taste

Salmon Croquettes

SALMON CROQUETTES

INGREDIENTS

½ lb. celery

½ lb. bell pepper

½ lb. onion

½ lb. butter

1 lb. crushed saltines

16 eggs

(8) 1 lb. cans of red salmon

vegetable oil

Customers, including my mother, thought Len Berg's made the best salmon croquettes they ever tasted. Amerson's cooks, who fried the patties so they were crunchy on the outside and tender on the inside, declared red salmon to be the secret to their great flavor.

DIRECTIONS

Chop fine ½ pound celery, ½ pound bell pepper, and ½ pound onion. Cook in ½ pound butter until tender.

Mix together 1 pound crushed saltines and 16 eggs; add the cooked vegetables and eight 1-pound cans red salmon, drained. Shape the mixture into balls or patties and fry in vegetable oil over medium heat until golden brown, about 2 minutes on each side or in a deep fryer until golden brown.

Filet Mignon

Len Berg's filet mignon was a traditional favorite from the time Berg put it on the menu through the Barry and Amerson years. Though Berg cut steaks himself, Amerson worked closely with slaughterhouses in Macon and Augusta to procure the best cuts of meat possible.

DIRECTIONS

Begin with a 5-ounce cut of steer tenderloin. Season with a blend of salt and pepper; wrap a strip of bacon around and secure with a toothpick. Broil or grill for the following times: Rare, 5 to 6 minutes; medium, 9 to 11 minutes; well done, 12 to 14 minutes.

Berg offered "Steak-in-the-Red" which was, as Buster Barry explained, a filet mignon topped with a small serving of chili ladled over the top.

FILET MIGNON

INGREDIENTS

5 oz. steer tenderloin

salt and pepper

bacon

chili (optional)

Macaroni and Cheese

MACARONI AND CHEESE

INGREDIENTS

1 lb. macaroni noodles

1 lb. shredded cheddar cheese

1 Tbsp. butter

1 C. powdered milk

1 Qt. water or milk

1 egg

Like many Southerners, Len Berg's sometimes took heat from food critics for considering this starchy dish a vegetable selection. Customers, though, were quite happy the comfort food was on the menu.

DIRECTIONS

Preheat oven to 325 degrees.

Follow package directions to prepare 1 pound of macaroni noodles in boiling water. Pour cooked noodles into a greased baking dish and stir in ½ pound shredded cheddar cheese. (mild or sharp according to taste preference). Stir in 1 tablespoon melted butter.

Mix together 1 cup powdered milk and 1 quart water (or 1 quart of milk), and 1 egg. Pour this over the macaroni and cheese mixture in the pan, making sure there is enough milk to rise to the top of the layer of noodles. Sprinkle another ½ pound of shredded cheddar over the top and bake, uncovered, for about one hour.

Fried Corn

The term "fried" corn often surprised new Len Berg's customers; the dish was closer to what many considered to be "creamed" corn. Len Berg's offered this vegetable on the menu every day because it was a perennial favorite.

DIRECTIONS

Starting with fresh produce, shuck and remove silks from 12 ears of corn. Hold an ear upright in a steady, deep pan or dish, and with a sharp knife, shave off kernels into the pan; using the back of the knife blade, scrape juices from the cob into the pan as well.

In a large, cast-iron skillet, melt 3 tablespoons butter over low heat, and stir in a small amount of flour or cornstarch to make a thin roux; add salt and pepper to taste. Add the corn kernels and juice to the pan and cook over low heat for 10 to 15 minutes.

FRIED CORN

INGREDIENTS

12 ears of corn

3 Tbsp. butter

flour or cornstarch

salt and pepper, to taste

Corn Sticks

CORN STICKS

INGREDIENTS

4 ½ lbs. yellow corn meal

4 ½ lbs. flour

1 C. baking powder

⅓ C. salt

3 C. sugar

3 C. powdered milk

6 eggs

1 C. wesson oil

2 Qts. cold water

Cornbread is a staple of Southern cooking, from thin lacy griddle cakes to the heartier mix baked in heavy cast-iron skillets. Len Berg's used special cast-iron baking pans to prepare individual corn muffins. Each muffin looked like a small stick of yellow corn. The soft, crunchy Corn Sticks held up well in the warming drawer, and those not served could be refrigerated and ground up to be used in cornbread dressing.

DIRECTIONS

Preheat oven to 400 degrees.

Prepare dry mix of 4 ½ pounds of yellow corn meal, 4 ½ pounds of flour, 1 cup baking powder, ⅓ cup salt, 3 cups sugar, and 3 cups powdered milk. This can be stored in an airtight container until ready to add wet ingredients and bake.

To ½ of this dry mixture, add 6 eggs and 1 cup Wesson oil. Mix well. Slowly pour in about 2 quarts cold water and mix well. Pour into greased cast-iron pans divided into sections for individual sticks of bread or into well-seasoned cast-iron muffin pans. Bake in a hot oven until brown on top (15 to 20 minutes).

A Second Helping

Boston Cream Pie

Like "Fried Corn" that wasn't fried, or orange-colored "Blue Cheese Dressing," Boston cream pie surprised many new Len Berg's diners. It was not really a pie at all, but rather, yellow cake with a vanilla-cream filling. Some people expected a chocolate frosting, but as they found, Len Berg's offered a version similar to that found in Wenzel's Menu Maker.

DIRECTIONS

Split a 10-inch layer of yellow cake in half horizontally. Spread 1 pint of vanilla-cream filling on the cut side of the top half; cover with the bottom half, cut side down. Sift powdered sugar over the top and slice.

Vanilla-cream filling is made by mixing 1 ¼ cups granulated sugar and ½ teaspoon salt in a saucepan. Add 2 ½ quarts of milk and 1 ounce of butter or margarine. Heat until the edges of the mixture bubble. Dissolve ¾ cup corn starch in ¾ cup milk and add ½ teaspoon yellow food coloring. Add to the cream mixture and stir briskly for 5 minutes until it becomes thick. Beat 8 eggs lightly and add a small amount of the hot milk mixture before turning the eggs back into the hot cream mix. Stir 2 minutes. Remove from heat; add ½ teaspoon vanilla extract and chill until needed in the Boston cream pie.

To serve, cut a wedge or a square piece and top with whipped cream.

BOSTON CREAM PIE

INGREDIENTS

10 inch layer of yellow cake

1 pint vanilla cream filling

powdered sugar

~~~~

Vanilla cream filling

1 ¼ C. granulated sugar

½ tsp. salt

2 ½ Qts. milk

1 oz. butter or margarine

¾ C. cornstarch

¾ C. milk

½ tsp. yellow food coloring

8 eggs

½ tsp. vanilla flavoring

~~~~

whipped cream

Cherry Cobbler

CHERRY COBBLER

INGREDIENTS

(3) 20 oz. cans of cherries

1 C. melted butter

2 C. sugar

1 Tbsp. nutmeg

cornstarch

pastry

whipped cream or vanilla ice cream

When the Keep Macon-Bibb County Beautiful Commission introduced the Cherry Blossom Festival in 1982, Jeff Amerson celebrated with the rest of the community. He directed Len Berg's cooks to top the "Macaroon Pie" with pink whipped cream, and he added cherry cobbler to the daily menu during the festival.

DIRECTIONS

Preheat oven to 400 degrees.

Drain three #2 (20 ounces) cans of cherries (about 2 ½ cups each), reserving the juice; pour the cherries into a greased baking dish (10- x 16-inch).

Mix with the reserved cherry juice, 1 cup melted butter, 2 cups sugar, and 1 tablespoon nutmeg. Len Berg's cooks suggested, "Add cornstarch to tighten the sauce if needed," indicating the sauce should have a moderate thickness. Pour the thickened sauce over the cherries and top with a favorite pastry. Bake in the oven for about 20 to 25 minutes until brown and bubbly.

Serve topped with a dollop of whipped cream or scoop of vanilla ice cream.

Turkey & Dressing

When Jerry Amerson married in 1979, his mother-in-law was delighted to learn about Len Berg's Restaurant's turkey and dressing orders "to go." Ida Jones focused her holiday preparations on baking pumpkin and pecan pies and left the main course to her "favorite son-in-law."

Chef Mitcham and the cooks at both Len Berg's locations spent hours mixing extra cornbread dressing and baking extra turkeys on the days before each year's holiday closings—all as they were still preparing for regular lunch-time crowds. They wrapped the turkeys (some people had them carve and slice it for them), and readied the dressing and giblet gravy with cooking instructions so cooks at home could pull out a piping hot pan of golden dressing to serve at their holiday meal.

DIRECTIONS

Follow the cooking times and instructions on a packaged fresh or frozen turkey with the following adaptations: Spread butter or oil over the turkey before placing it in a pan with about 1 to 2 inches of water in the bottom. Season with salt and pepper, and sprinkle granulated chicken bouillon over the top of the bird. Add chunks of onion and celery around the bird, cover, and bake. During the final 30 minutes of baking, remove the cover so the bird can brown a bit.

Remove the turkey from the pan and strain the broth to use in preparing the dressing and gravy.

Instructions for Cornbread dressing on following page.

TURKEY & DRESSING

INGREDIENTS

fresh or frozen turkey

butter or oil

salt and pepper

granulated chicken bouillon

water

onion

celery

~~~~

INGREDIENTS

Cornbread dressing:

½ lb. celery

½ lb. onion

1 to 2 Tbsp. butter

3 C. flour or ground rolls

3 C. cornmeal or ground corn sticks

8 eggs

1 ½ Qts. chicken stock

melted butter, to drizzle

Gravy:

¼ C. butter

1 to 2 Tbsp. flour

1 C. broth

pepper, to taste

2 tsp. chicken bouillon

1 boiled egg

cooked turkey giblets or turkey

CORNBREAD DRESSING:

Len Berg's cornbread dressing was made with leftover corn sticks and rolls that were stored in the freezer or refrigerator until ready for use. The bread was ground up to a fine texture, and if there was not enough, corn meal or flour was added.

Begin by chopping fine ½ pound celery and ½ pound of onion; place in saucepan with 1 to 2 tablespoons of butter and cook over medium-high heat until the vegetables are soft. In a large bowl, mix together 3 cups flour (or ground rolls) and 3 cups cornmeal (or ground corn sticks). Add 8 eggs, beaten, and stir in the celery and onion mix. Add 1 ½ quarts of chicken stock. You can use the pan drippings from the baked turkey for this, but reserve at least 1 to 2 cups for the gravy. Pour the soupy dressing mixture into a greased baking dish, drizzle with melted butter, and bake in a 400-degree preheated oven for about one hour or until golden brown on top.

GRAVY:

The gravy begins with ¼ cup butter melted in a saucepan; whisk in 1 to 2 tablespoons of flour to form a roux. When the roux is smooth and lightly colored, add 1 cup broth (pan drippings or chicken broth), pepper to taste, and 2 teaspoons of chicken bouillon. Stir in a chopped boiled egg. You can also add cooked turkey giblets or small pieces of the cooked turkey to provide additional flavor and texture to the gravy.

Fried Oysters

An ad or card on the table stating "Oysters 'R' in Season" offered a reminder for customers when they could order fried oysters at Len Berg's. The restaurant served the seafood only during the traditional season, from September through April, avoiding the hot summer months of May, June, July, and August.

DIRECTIONS

Oysters were prepared for frying by patting them dry before dredging in a mixture of 1 quart flour, 1 quart cornstarch, 2 quarts cracker meal, and 1 tablespoon each of salt and pepper. Drop the coated oysters in a deep fryer to cook to a golden brown, then serve immediately.

FRIED OYSTERS
INGREDIENTS
oysters
1 Qt. flour
1 Qt. cornstarch
2 Qts. cracker meal
1 Tbsp. salt
1 Tbsp. pepper
frying oil

Stuffed Shrimp

STUFFED SHRIMP

INGREDIENTS

Crabmeat stuffing:

1 lb. cooked crabmeat

½ C. chopped bell pepper

1 C. onion

2 oz. mushrooms

1 C. cracker meal

2 C. milk

3 eggs

10 drops Tabasco sauce

1 tsp. Worcestershire sauce

1 tsp. salt

½ tsp. pepper

~~~~

Jumbo shrimp, deveined

1 : 1 : 2 ratio of flour, cornstarch, and cracker meal

salt and pepper, to taste

Jerry Amerson's favorite dinner was an order of stuffed shrimp, baked potato, and a salad, which was also a popular selection for his customers. This dish requires a brief period in the freezer, so don't wait until the last moment to begin preparing. (This crabmeat mixture is also used in stuffed flounder, a recipe that appears in a later chapter.)

DIRECTIONS

The crabmeat stuffing is a mixture of 1 pound cooked crabmeat, ½ cup chopped bell pepper, 1 cup onion, 2 ounces mushrooms, 1 cup cracker meal, 2 cups regular milk, 3 whole eggs, 10 drops Tabasco, 1 teaspoon Worcestershire sauce, 1 teaspoon salt, and ½ teaspoon pepper. Refrigerate until ready to use.

Devein several jumbo shrimp and split them open to look like a butterfly. Put 1 tablespoon of crabmeat stuffing into the split and press the shrimp closed. Place several on a wax paper-lined sheet and put in the freezer at least 30 minutes before continuing.

Remove stuffed shrimp from freezer, and thaw if necessary. Dredge the shrimp in a mixture of 1 part flour, 1 part corn starch, 2 parts cracker meal, and salt and pepper to taste. Fry the breaded shrimp in deep fat until golden.

Carrot & Raisin Salad or Cole Slaw

Each day, Len Berg's lunch menu featured a cold salad as the final letter of the alphabet. Z always represented either cole slaw or carrot and raisin Salad.

DIRECTIONS

For carrot and raisin salad, wash, peel, and shred 5 pounds of raw carrots and mix with 1 cup raisins, 2 cups mayonnaise, ½ cup sugar, and 1 cup crushed pineapple. Chill and serve.

Cole slaw was a mix of 5 pounds of shredded cabbage, 1 raw carrot, ½ tablespoon salt, 2 cups mayonnaise, 1 cup sweet pickle relish, and ½ cup pickle juice. Chill and serve.

INGREDIENTS

Carrot and raisin salad:

5 lbs. raw carrots

1 C. raisins

2 C. mayonnaise

½ C. sugar

1 C. crushed pineapple

~~~~

Cole slaw:

5 lbs. shredded cabbage

1 grated carrot

½ Tbsp. salt

2 C. mayonnaise

1 C. pickle relish

½ C. sweet pickle juice

Fried Apples

FRIED APPLES

INGREDIENTS

Batter:

2 Qts. flour

½ C. sugar

2 Tbsp. baking powder

1 Tbsp. vanilla extract

1 Tbsp. cinnamon

cold water

~~~~

cooking apples

granulated sugar

Some customers ordered fried apples along with their entree and other vegetables, but saved them for dessert. Jerry Amerson recalled how one customer often made a meal of one order of fried corn and three orders of fried apples.

DIRECTIONS

In a large bowl, mix together 2 quarts flour, ½ cup sugar, 2 tablespoons baking powder, 1 tablespoon vanilla extract, and 1 tablespoon cinnamon. Add cold water to make a medium batter (resembles a thin pancake batter).

Peel, core, and slice firm, cooking apples (York or Rome work best for this recipe). Dip apple slices in the batter and fry until golden. Drain and immediately sprinkle with granulated sugar before serving.

Southern Succotash

This medley of Southern vegetables was not on the menu often, but Jerry Amerson recalled how his father, among others, often ordered fried corn, baby limas, and tomatoes and okra, and then mixed it together on his plate. A collection of information from Len Berg's included a note about the ingredients for Southern Succotash, but the dish was certainly one for which the master cooks at Len Berg's really did not need a recipe.

DIRECTIONS

Combine 1 pound of peeled, seeded, and chopped tomatoes with 1 cup sliced okra, 1 teaspoon salt, a dash of freshly ground pepper, and 2 tablespoons minced celery. Cover pan and simmer vegetables 5 minutes. Add 1 cup fresh lima beans and simmer for 15 minutes more. Add a little chicken stock if necessary. Add 1 cup freshly scraped corn pulp and simmer for 8 mins or until tender. Add 2 tablespoons butter, salt and pepper to taste, and serve hot.

SOUTHERN SUCCOTASH

INGREDIENTS

1 lb. peeled, seeded, chopped tomatoes

1 C. sliced okra

1 tsp. salt

freshly ground pepper

2 Tbsp. minced celery

1 C. fresh lima beans

chicken stock

1 C. corn pulp

2 Tbsp. butter

Vegetable Soup

VEGETABLE SOUP

INGREDIENTS

12 to 13 C. canned tomatoes

2 C. canned whole kernel corn or fresh corn

¾ lb. sliced carrots

¾ lb. chopped celery

½ lb. sliced or chopped onion

2 C. cooked rice

1 ½ lbs. chopped potatoes

½ lb. browned beef tips

½ lb. chopped bell pepper

In the South, vegetable soup was often based on foods available in the family garden. At a restaurant, it offered an opportunity for cooks to use up small portions of meat or vegetables left in the pot at the end of a shift. Len Berg's waitresses were always amused when their customers ordered soup and stressed, "Be sure my vegetable soup has a piece of meat in it."

DIRECTIONS

Combine one #10 (108 ounces/13 cups) can of tomatoes (12 to 13 cups), one #303 (17 ounces/2 cups) can of whole kernel corn (or 2 cups of fresh corn), ¾ pound sliced carrots, ¾ pound chopped celery, ½ pound sliced/chopped onion, 2 cups rice (cooked), 1 ½ pounds chopped potatoes, ½ pound browned beef tips; ½ pound chopped bell pepper. Bring to a boil for 5 to 10 minutes, reduce heat, and simmer until vegetables are tender and ready to serve.

Beets in Orange Sauce

Even picky eaters learned to like beets when they ate Len Berg's version of the root vegetable.

DIRECTIONS

In a saucepan, mix 1 cup sugar, 2 tablespoons cornstarch, 1 teaspoon salt, 4 tablespoons water, 1 cup vinegar. Bring to a boil, stirring until the mixture clears. Add the rind and juice of 2 oranges, and 6 tablespoons of butter.

Drain one #10 (109 ounces/13 cups) can of beets (12 to 13 cups) and heat in a saucepan over low heat. Strain the orange sauce, pour over the beets, and keep warm until serving.

BEETS IN ORANGE SAUCE

INGREDIENTS

Orange sauce:

1 C. sugar

2 Tbsp. cornstarch

1 tsp. salt

4 Tbsp. water

1 C. vinegar

rind and juice of 2 oranges

6 Tbsp. butter

~~~~

12 to 13 C. of canned beets

Lemon Meringue Pie

Customers sometimes scheduled their lunch dates on the basis of whether it was lemon- or chocolate-pie day at Len Berg's. They knew chocolate meringue pie was on the menu on Tuesday, Thursday, and Saturday and that lemon meringue pie appeared on Monday, Wednesday, and Friday.

Local printers Smith & Watson prepared new menus each month when Len Berg's made changes to the items they offered. Once, when the days for lemon and chocolate pies got switched, the Amersons thought they might have to order new menus sooner than usual in order to keep customers happy about their dining schedule!

DIRECTIONS

Pastry (for two pies):

Sift 2 ½ cups flour with 1 teaspoon salt. Work in 4 tablespoons baking powder and 4 tablespoons butter until mixture is mealy. Moisten only enough to hold together with 4 to 6 tablespoons of ice water. Form into two balls and keep cold until used. Roll out each ball lightly and cover two pie pans. Cut off all but about 2 inch overhang. Pinch the overhang onto the edge of the pan and crimp with floured fingers. Jab entire surface with fork to prevent puffing. Bake 15 to 20 minutes at 450 to 500 degrees until lightly browned.

Filling (for two pies):

Preheat oven to 350 degrees. Grate lemons for 2 tablespoons of lemon rind. Cut and squeeze lemons through a strainer for ½ cup lemon juice; set aside.

Mix in the top of a large enamel double boiler, 1 cup minus 2 tablespoons corn starch, 3 cups sugar; gradually add 3 cups boiling water, stirring continuously. Cook over direct heat, always stirring, until thick and boiling. Then, still stirring, place the top and bottom of the double boiler together and cook the syrup over boiling water 10 minutes more. In a small bowl, beat 6 egg yolks lightly and add to mixture still stirring; add 6 tablespoons butter and stir until melted. Add ½ cup strained lemon juice and 2 tablespoons grated lemon rind. Stir well and remove from boiling water to cool. Pour into two pre-baked shells.

Meringue (for two pies):

In a large bowl, beat whites of 6 eggs with 1 ½ teaspoons cream of tartar until they just hold a peak. Gradually add ¾ cup of sugar and 2 teaspoons vanilla extract. Pile lightly on two pies, being sure the meringue touches pastry all the way around and covers the filling to prevent bleeding. Bake at 350 degrees for about 10 minutes or until lightly browned.

LEMON MERINGUE PIE

INGREDIENTS

Filling:

2 Tbsp. lemon rind, grated

½ C. lemon juice

1 C. (minus 2 Tbsp.) cornstarch

3 C. sugar

3 C. boiling water

6 egg yolks, lightly beaten

6 Tbsp. butter

~ ~ ~

Meringue:

6 egg whites

1 ½ tsp. cream of tartar

¾ C. sugar

2 tsp. vanilla extract

MENU

THE ORIGINAL

Len Berg's

RESTAURANT

FAMOUS FOR FINE FOOD

SINCE 1908

Sea Foods

Steaks and Chops

Fried Chicken

Italian Spaghetti

Post Office Alley, Macon, Ga.

CHAPTER SIX

Friday Night Specials

Closing the doors of Len Berg's Restaurant meant patrons would move on to new places, but it did not diminish their fondness for the food and people of an establishment that served Macon for almost 100 years. Following Leonard Berg's tenure, Art Barry owned the restaurant for twenty-five years, then the Amerson family owned it for another thirty-five years. The restaurant served several thousand people each week, so there is little wonder that Jerry Amerson and Buster Berry recalled many stories from their days of growing up in the business. Friday nights seemed to evoke a certain flavor of favorite stories.

When Art Barry still owned Len Berg's in the 1960s, it was not unusual for patrons to discretely bring in their favorite adult beverages to enjoy with a meal. Early one Friday night, Barry was working alongside his assistant manager, Jeff Amerson, when they seated such a group in Room 3. The diners enjoyed a boisterous meal and left for another engagement by 7:30 PM.

Bus boys quickly cleared the table to set the room up for another large group that was "in the house" and ready to be seated. They delivered dirty dishes to the kitchen, and Lula, the dishwasher, went to work. Instead of emptying the glasses into the sink, Lula poured the remaining liquids into one glass to drink as she ran pots and pans and dishes through the wash.

A short while later, Barry heard a loud crash and rushed into the kitchen to find a tipsy dishwasher and a floor scattered with broken plates and glasses. The owner fired Lula on the spot, explaining to her and all his staff that he would not tolerate such behavior. Barry struggled to escort Lula out of the kitchen as she slurred, "Aw, Mr. B. You can't fire me. I loves you."

Barry left the restaurant in the capable hands of his assistant manager, Jeff Amerson, and drove the dishwasher to her residence. Since the night was still young, he went home to pick up his wife, Texas, and returned to the restaurant for a late dinner. When the couple entered the building, Barry's assistant manager greeted him with a grin. Amerson seated Mrs. Barry, then asked the owner to step into the kitchen. Barry swung open the narrow double doors and was greeted by a smiling Lula at her station washing dishes. She looked up from the dishwater and shouted, "Hey Mr. B. I'm so happy to see you!"

Barry may not have been happy to see Lula, but he allowed her to stay on as dishwasher the rest of that night and for many more years.

Lula remained in the position, even after Jeff Amerson took over as owner in 1969; he reminded her, though, to stay away from alcohol as she washed dishes or helped the baker and other cooks as needed. He also continued to allow customers to brown-bag adult beverages until he obtained a license to sell beer.

The restaurant owner did not worry about his patrons drinking too much; as customers celebrated with friends, Amerson encouraged them to eat plenty of hearty food to help counter the effects of alcohol. He did have to worry, though, about a few individuals who spent their Friday paycheck at a downtown liquor store, then stumbled through the restaurant parking lot on their way to someplace else. Such passersby were usually only a nuisance, but one of them cost Amerson a car.

One Friday after lunch, Amerson took a deposit to the bank and got change for his assistant manager to use during the evening's dinner shift. Amerson returned from the bank and left his '68 Chevy Impala station wagon idling in front of the empty restaurant. As he and the assistant manager stood at the counter going over details about the expected Friday evening rush, Amerson heard a car door slam. He looked up in time to see his seafoam green station wagon take off down the alley. Amerson ran out to the parking lot and watched his car scrape the side of the Macon Blueprint building on the corner as the driver turned right on Walnut Street and disappeared. Police later confirmed that the inebriated driver crashed into two cars and a city bus before trying to abandon Amerson's car two blocks away on Broadway.

Of course, Friday night celebrations did not always include alcohol. Families often gathered on Friday or Saturday nights for someone's birthday or other special occasion. The group usually indulged in a piece of hot fudge cake that was presented to the guest of honor or they ordered one of the other popular desserts to finish off the celebratory meal.

In the 1970s, Jerry Amerson was working as assistant manager one Friday evening when a group made an entire meal of desserts. At the time, Delta Airlines offered several daily flights into and out of Macon, and Amerson seated a group of six pilots, all dressed in their Delta uniforms. The men did not order Len Berg's famous filet mignon, stuffed flounder, or stuffed shrimp. They did not order a salad or potatoes or onion rings. Instead, the pilots asked the waiter to bring them one of every dessert on the menu! Each man ordered macaroon pie, strawberry shortcake, apple pie, hot fudge cake a la mode, *and* lemon meringue pie. As the waiter wrote out the orders, he asked if the men wanted their apple pie served warm with ice cream or with melted cheese on top. One pilot answered that he wanted his apple pie with cheese and ice cream and hot fudge sauce, too. Then the other five men in the party ordered the same!

Len Berg's, macaroon pie was the only dessert served on what was my most memorable Friday night special. Before Jerry began working full-time at the restaurant, he took me there for our first date in 1978. The booths and tables were already filled, so we sat at the counter for a quick dinner before we went to see a movie. We had fried shrimp and sides, and then, since I had never heard of macaroon pie, Jerry encouraged me to give it a try. Little did I know then how many pieces of macaroon pie and other desserts

Family celebrating graduation at Len Berg's. Seated from left to right: Ellen Ewing (Gutermuth), Jacqueline Souder (Cates), Ruthanna Ewing, R.C. Souder, Josh Ewing (c. June 1978).

and meals I would enjoy from Len Berg's over the next twenty-five years!

In the two and one-half decades of my association with Len Berg's, I sat at the same counter and observed how the restaurant's patrons often had their favorite waiter or waitress. Some patrons had a favorite booth or table. People had a favorite time of day to dine at the restaurant. Some enjoyed the hustle and bustle of a crowd at noon; some rushed in at the last possible moment before the kitchen closed; and some rushed to beat the crowd by being first through the door for lunch or dinner.

I saw that the wait staff knew their customers well, knew which ones wanted tea or coffee, and I learned that they served up more than food on a plate. The waitress at the counter on Saturday knew her first customer of the day would order only fried corn and the potato of the day, and that when the plate was put down in front of him, the elderly gentleman would pour out at least half of the sugar container onto his food. Worried about the health effects of an extra cup of sugar on top of corn and potatoes, the waitress began to start her Saturday shift with a half-filled sugar container at that end of the counter. She hoped to help the man consume less sugar and knew he would not ask for more if he emptied the container. The waitress would likely have time to refill the sugar container later in the day.

Saturdays were a bit more casual than other days, a welcome relief after the lunch rushes during the week and the excitement of Friday nights. The kitchen and wait staff could hope for an easier pace except on Saturday evenings in the fall when the University of Georgia football team played an early game at home in Athens. If the game ended by 4:00 PM, fans rushed home to Macon and headed

straight to Len Berg's to order filet mignon, baked potato, and a salad with Epic dressing before the restaurant closed at 10:00 PM. Patrons wearing red and black filled the halls as they waited for a table, and the atmosphere reflected whether the UGA bulldogs had won or lost the game.

Everyone at Len Berg's appreciated the slower pace of Saturdays, and it was especially welcomed by one of the older waitresses, Ruby. (Jerry Amerson explained that Ruby was "old" when he became assistant manager in 1978, "and she stayed old." He recalled how the other waitresses could not determine Ruby's age and laughed about her mumbling an answer whenever they discussed the topic.) On Saturdays Ruby could focus on serving a sweet couple absorbed in one another instead of the impatient businessman who snapped at her for moving too slowly. Jeff Amerson defended his waitress by asking the man, "Did you want it in a hurry or do you want it on a plate?"

No matter their age, the waitresses, waiters, and kitchen staff welcomed Saturday's relative ease. Then they savored Sunday, a day of rest, before starting all over again on Monday when Macon's downtown returned to its weekday activities. All of Len Berg's staff returned to routines on Monday. They managed the many details of a busy restaurant, the unseen hustle of morning preparations, ordering food, shucking corn, baking bread and pies, and all the tasks needed to serve good food to their customers. After all, freshly prepared food was the reason people came to the little red brick building in the alley.

Previous chapters of this book offered recipes for Len Berg's foods served during the Berg, Barry, and Amerson eras. This chapter features additional recipes for perennial favorites.

I think Rick Bragg, who wrote a book about how his mother prepared food, might understand the challenges I faced with trying to document recipes from the restaurant. To a natural cook like Bragg's mother, Margaret, as well as the cooks at Len Berg's, cooking good food was a skill learned over many years. Recipes were not always written; the cook just observed the sounds and smells and feel of the kitchen to know when the food was ready to serve. It was done when it was done. My mother was also a natural cook, but I did not inherit her skills and ease in the kitchen. For non-cooks like me, we need a bit more than a simple list of ingredients. I often flip through various cookbooks or browse the internet for information about putting ingredients together or for advice on how long to cook a particular dish.

Before our family sold the restaurant in 2003, I typed up "recipes" from notes my father-in-law, Jeff Amerson, had collected through the years. The notes resulted from times when he and Art Barry directed the cooks to compile a list of ingredients and measurements for each item. The owners used the information to calculate food costs for single servings, a critical tool for determining if or when to adjust prices on the menu.

Len Berg's cooks generally worked from memory and their natural sense of preparing food daily. On the occasion of listing ingredients for the owner, they slowed down to measure, but rarely did they include information about the process of combining ingredients or specifics about cooking temperature or the length of time something baked. The compilation of notes included at least seven different "recipes" for pastry: one from Mary Dee was enough to make twelve crusts for chocolate and lemon pie; another made eight crusts; one indicated it was pastry for six apple pies; another made pastry for twenty crusts; and so on. No two recipes were the same, even if I tried to do the math to reduce or increase the amount of ingredients. When I wanted to bake a pie, I had to go to another another source for a recipe and hope the pastry held up well for the filling I used.

Because I am someone who does not cook often, I did not test each of the following recipes for accuracy. (Remember my resumé from Len Berg's—I was a taster, not a cook.) I did not have the Strongboy flour or Arnett's corn meal, and I don't usually have powdered whole milk or a five-pound box of Pillsbury yellow cake mix on hand. I tried to reduce some of the recipes to a family-sized batch, and I provided basic steps for these recipes. But when in doubt about how to proceed with any of these, please do as I did when I wanted to make a single pie crust—visit your favorite cookbook or website for more information.

I wish you great success as you make your favorite dish from this book. And I hope you will remember not only the food, but also the people who made Len Berg's Restaurant a perennial favorite place to dine.

Marie J. Amerson inside Len Berg's Carryout during construction. (October 1987)

A Second Helping

A Second Helping of Recipes

Apple Pie Filling

Baked Stuffed Flounder

Banana Pudding

Black-eyed Peas

Boiled New Potatoes

Candied Sweet Potatoes

Chocolate Pie Filling

Chicken Pan Pie

Hard Rolls

Hot Fudge Cake a la Mode

Peach Cobbler

Peaches and Cream Pie

Pineapple Upsidedown Cake

Strawberry Shortcake

Tomatoes and Okra

HAPPY BIRTHDAY!
This card entitles you to a **FREE LUNCH**
at
LEN BERG'S
(Not to exceed Five Dollars)

MONDAYS THRU FRIDAYS 11:15 til 3 P.M.
COMPLIMENTS OF

A business card announcing a birthday treat. (c. 1979)

Apple Pie

Many customers ordered their pie "a la mode" with a scoop of vanilla ice cream. During peach season, a scoop of H.M.F.P.I.C. seemed to add the right touch for some patrons. Jerry Amerson recalled that Mr. Holloway, a part-time host at the restaurant, enjoyed a slice with melted cheese and called it "applus" pie.

DIRECTIONS

Combine 12 cups sliced apples, 9 tablespoons cornstarch, 3 cups granulated sugar, 2 ½ teaspoons cinnamon, ¼ teaspoon nutmeg, and ¼ cup butter; cook on stovetop over medium heat to soften the apples and thicken the mixture. Remove from heat and spoon the filling evenly into four deep pastry shells. Layer strips of pastry across the top.

Bake at 350 degrees until brown, about 45 to 60 minutes.

APPLE PIE

INGREDIENTS

Pastry for four double-crust pies

1 #10 can (12 cups) White House sliced apples

9 Tbsp. cornstarch

3 C. granulated sugar

2 ½ tsp. cinnamon

¼ tsp. nutmeg

¼ C. butter

Makes four pies

Baked Stuffed Flounder

BAKED STUFFED FLOUNDER

INGREDIENTS

Crabmeat Stuffing

1 lb. cooked crabmeat

½ C. chopped bell pepper

1 C. onion, chopped

2 oz. mushrooms

1 C. cracker meal

2 C. milk

3 eggs

10 drops Tabasco sauce

1 tsp. Worcestershire sauce

1 tsp. salt

½ tsp. pepper

~~~

Flounder, 1 lb. or less

This menu item used the same crab mixture as the stuffed shrimp, but offered a baked alternative.

DIRECTIONS

The crabmeat stuffing is a mixture of 1 pound cooked crabmeat, ½ cup chopped bell pepper, 1 cup chopped onion, 2 ounces mushrooms, 1 cup cracker meal, 2 cups regular milk, 3 whole eggs, 10 drops Tabasco, 1 teaspoon Worcestershire sauce, 1 teaspoon salt, and ½ teaspoon pepper. Refrigerate until ready to use in flounder or shrimp.

Remove skin from the top of the flounder; make a slit on top and stuff with ¼ to ½ cup of the crabmeat stuffing. Wrap in foil and bake in 400 degree oven for 15 minutes.

Banana Pudding

Len Berg's cooks knew that true Southern-style banana pudding was a cooked custard, bananas, and a meringue baked to a golden glow.

DIRECTIONS

Combine ½ cup sugar, 2 tablespoons flour, and ¼ teaspoon salt in a heavy saucepan. Beat 3 egg yolks and mix well with 2 cups milk. Stir liquids into the dry mixture and cook over medium heat, stirring constantly, until smooth and thickened. Remove from heat; stir in 1 teaspoon vanilla.

Layer vanilla wafers in the bottom and along the sides of a 3-quart baking dish. Slice bananas and layer over wafers. Pour the cooled custard over the top. (You may divide the ingredients to assemble the pudding into layers of custard, bananas, and wafers.)

Meringue:

Beat 3 egg whites (at room temperature) until foamy. Gradually add ½ teaspoon cream of tartar and ½ cup granulated sugar, beating until stiff peaks form. Add 1 teaspoon vanilla.

Spread meringue over custard, sealing to the edge of the baking dish. Bake at 425 degrees for 10 to 12 minutes or until golden brown.

BANANA PUDDING

INGREDIENTS

½ C. sugar

2 Tbsp. all-purpose flour

¼ tsp. salt

2 C. milk

3 eggs, separated

1 tsp. vanilla extract

6 ripe bananas

1 box vanilla wafers (11 oz.)

Meringue:

3 egg whites

½ tsp. cream of tartar

½ C. granulated sugar

1 tsp. vanilla extract

Black-eyed Peas

BLACK-EYED PEAS

INGREDIENTS

2 C. dried black-eyed peas

½ pound fatback

¼ C. chopped onion

1 Tbsp. butter

1 Tbsp. salt

1 Tbsp. black pepper

1 sprig parsley, chopped

Traditionally, folks in the South expect to eat black-eyed peas and rice on January 1. Len Berg's Restaurant helped its patrons ring in the New Year with a complimentary serving of black-eyed peas so everyone could find good fortune in the year to come.

DIRECTIONS

Sort and wash 2 cups of dried black-eyed peas, then place in pan of hot water to soak (2 hours). Drain.

Boil ½ pound fatback, ¼ cup chopped onion, 1 tablespoon butter, 1 tablespoon salt, 1 tablespoon ground black pepper, and a sprig of parsley in 2 quarts of water for about 10 minutes, then add drained peas and simmer for 2 hours or until the peas are tender and the water has cooked very low.

Boiled New Potatoes

The potato dish of the day was always indicated by the letter "K" and when this simple dish was seasoned just right, it made a hearty side to meat loaf or minced steak. (Or, if you are like the Saturday customer mentioned earlier in this chapter, potatoes and corn seasoned with a cup of sugar could make an entire meal!)

DIRECTIONS

Peel 2 pounds of potatoes and place in heavy saucepan with enough water to cover; add 1 tablespoon salt. Boil rapidly for 5 minutes, then simmer for another 10 minutes. Drain the stock but save 1 quart to mix with ½ cup butter and a drop of yellow food coloring. Bring to a boil and thicken with cornstarch.

Pour over the cooked potatoes and sprinkle chopped parsley over the top.

BOILED NEW POTATOES

INGREDIENTS

2 lbs. small red potatoes

water

1 Tbsp. salt

½ C. butter

drop yellow food coloring

cornstarch

parsley, chopped

Candied Sweet Potatoes

CANDIED SWEET POTATOES

INGREDIENTS

10 lb. sweet potatoes

3 C. sugar

1 ½ tsp. cinnamon

1 tsp. nutmeg

1 qt. water

1 lemon

½ C. butter

#2 can (2 ½ c.) White House sliced apples

Waiters and waitresses knew patrons were not local when they identified this dish as "candied yams."

DIRECTIONS

Cover sweet potatoes with water and boil 30 minutes. Cool, drain, peel, and slice.

Mix 3 cups sugar, 1 ½ teaspoon cinnamon, and 1 teaspoon nutmeg with 1 quart water in a saucepan; add juice from 1 lemon and ½ cup butter cut into small pieces. Cook over medium high heat until sugar dissolves, stirring constantly until syrup thickens slightly.

In a buttered baking pan, arrange sliced sweet potatoes and 2 ½ c. canned apple slices. Pour syrup over all and bake at 350 degrees for 15 minutes or until the mixture is bubbly.

Chicken Pan Pie

One of my favorite selections at Len Berg's was their version of chicken pot pie which came steaming hot from the kitchen in an individual white ramekin. The notes for this suggested the cooks might also have prepared the savory pie in a large baking pan. And though it was called "chicken" pan pie, the secret ingredient was actually turkey.

DIRECTIONS

Heat 2 quarts of chicken broth over medium heat and thicken with a bit of cornstarch or flour; add 1 tablespoon butter. Combine 2 ½ cups bite-sized pieces of turkey with 1 ½ cups cooked and diced potatoes and carrots; stir in ½ cup cooked English peas and 3 diced boiled eggs. Stir the mixture into thickened chicken broth; salt and pepper to taste. Pour the soupy mixture into 13- x 9- x 2-inch baking dish, or spoon into individual baking dishes. Top with pastry and cut slits to allow steam to escape.

Bake at 400 degrees for 30 minutes or until brown.

CHICKEN PAN PIE

INGREDIENTS

Pastry

2 qt. chicken broth

1 Tbsp. flour or cornstarch

1 Tbsp. butter

2 1/2 C. cooked turkey, diced

1 ½ C. cooked and diced potatoes and carrots

½ C. English peas

3 hard boiled eggs, diced

salt and pepper to taste

Chocolate Pie Filling

CHOCOLATE PIE FILLING

INGREDIENTS

Pastry for one pie

1 c. granulated sugar

3 eggs, separated

3 Tbsp. flour

dash salt

3 Tbsp. cocoa

2 C. milk

1 Tbsp. butter

1 tsp. vanilla extract

~~~~

Meringue:

3 egg whites

½ tsp. cream of tartar

½ C. granulated sugar

1 tsp. vanilla extract

Many of Len Berg's customers had a favorite day to dine based on whether it was the day for Lemon Meringue Pie or Chocolate Meringue Pie. The notes from the kitchen indicated this pie filling might also have been used for individual servings of pudding when it was spooned into custard dishes, chilled, and served with a dollop of whipped cream.

DIRECTIONS

Preheat oven to 350 degrees.

Stir together in a heavy saucepan 1 cup sugar and 3 egg yolks; add 3 tablespoons flour, dash salt, and 3 tablespoons cocoa. Gradually stir in 2 cups milk and cook over medium heat, stirring constantly. Allow the mixture to come to a boil and cook for about 5 minutes until the mixture is smooth and thickened. Remove from heat; add in 1 tablespoon butter and 1 teaspoon vanilla and stir until butter melts. Spoon mixture into pastry shell.

Meringue:

Beat 3 egg whites (at room temperature) until foamy. Gradually add ½ teaspoon cream of tartar and ½ cup granulated sugar and beat to form peaks. Add 1 teaspoon vanilla and beat until stiff peaks form. Spread meringue over custard, sealing to the edge of the baking dish. Bake at 350 degrees for 10 to 12 minutes or until golden brown.

Slice this pie with a knife that has been dipped in ice water before each cut to help prevent tearing the meringue.

Hard Rolls

Bread choices at lunchtime were warm, yeasty cloverleaf rolls or corn sticks. At night, biscuits and hard rolls were also an option. The hard rolls topped with poppy seeds were a great accompaniment to the filet mignon and other steaks.

DIRECTIONS

Warm mixing bowl before adding 2 cups warm water, 4 teaspoons sugar, and 2 ounces of yeast. Stir to dissolve and let stand for 5 minutes. Gradually add 2 ½ cups warm water, 1 tablespoon salt, 3 tablespoons shortening, 1 teaspoon lemon juice, 1 egg white, and 5 to 6 cups all-purpose flour. Knead lightly. Let rise to double (about 2 hours at 80 degrees). Punch dough down and let it rest 10 minutes.

Cut off pieces of dough about the size of a walnut and roll it into balls; place the rolls on a pan that has been dusted with cornmeal and allow them to rise to double in size. (Len Berg's bakers had a special utensil that allowed them to create a swirl in the dough as they shaped the rolls.) Brush the tops with a mixture of egg white and water; sprinkle with poppy seeds.

Place a pan of water alongside the rolls and bake at 400 degrees for 25 to 30 minutes or until golden brown.

HARD ROLLS

INGREDIENTS

2 C. warm water

4 tsp. sugar

2 oz. yeast

2 ½ C. warm water

1 Tbsp. salt

3 Tbsp. shortening

1 tsp. lemon juice

1 egg white

5-6 C. all-purpose flour

~~~~~

1 egg white

water

poppy seeds

Hot Fudge Cake a la Mode

HOT FUDGE CAKE A LA MODE

INGREDIENTS

Fudge Sauce:

1 C. granulated sugar

1 ½ Tbsp. cocoa

1 C. whole milk

½ C. butter

½ tsp. vanilla extract

~~~~
**Cake:**

1 box Pillsbury yellow cake mix

eggs, vegetable oil, and water

~~~~
vanilla ice cream, sliced

This popular dessert was on the menu every day, handy to deliver on a special tray that played "Happy Birthday" when requested. Even without a request, the birthday treats were delivered sometimes because staff checked a special ledger near the cash register where they found a listing of birthdays for many of their regular customers.

DIRECTIONS

Fudge Sauce:

Mix 1 cup sugar and 1 ½ tablespoons cocoa well in a heavy saucepan; gradually add 1 cup whole milk and cook over medium heat, stirring often. Allow the mixture to boil for 5 to 10 minutes until it thickens; add ½ cup butter that has been cut into chunks. Remove from heat and add ½ teaspoon vanilla extract. Simmering the sauce longer will allow it to thicken, but the mixture should be cooled before pouring over the cake or ice cream. If the sauce becomes too thick, add more milk as needed.

Cake:

Prepare cake mix and bake as directed on the package. Remove from oven to cool, then remove from the pan. Cut a serving-size piece of cake, then split it horizontally.

Place a slice of vanilla ice cream between the layers of cake. (Len Berg's ordered individually wrapped slices of vanilla ice cream to use in the center of the hot fudge cake a la mode.)

Pour warm fudge sauce over the top of the cake allowing it to drizzle down the sides.

Peach Cobbler

The Len Berg's menu offered more than a half dozen dessert choices each day. A fruit cobbler was a popular choice, and peach was one of my favorites.

DIRECTIONS

Preheat oven to 350 degrees. Put ½ cup butter in a 9- x 13-inch baking dish and place in the oven to melt the butter. Mix together 1 cup flour, 1 ½ teaspoons baking powder, and ½ teaspoon salt; stir in 1 cup milk and 1 cup sugar to make a batter. Remove baking dish with melted butter from the oven and pour the batter in. Spoon 2 cups sliced peaches and their juice evenly over the batter.

Bake at 350 degrees for 30 minutes or until the batter is browned and has risen up around the fruit.

PEACH COBBLER

INGREDIENTS

½ C. butter

1 C. all-purpose flour

1 ½ tsp baking powder

½ tsp salt

1 C. milk

1 C. sugar

2 C. fresh or frozen peach slices

Peaches and Cream Pie

Pastry

¾ C. granulated sugar

½ C. all-purpose flour

2 C. peaches, sliced

1 C. heavy cream

This particular dessert was never on the menu at Len Berg's, but Jerry Amerson is sure that if his father had tasted it, Jeff Amerson would have added the creamy pie to satisfy patrons when H.M.F.P.I.C. was not available. It can be served warm, but Jerry prefers it chilled.

DIRECTIONS

Preheat oven to 350 degrees. Mix ¾ cup granulated sugar and ½ cup all-purpose flour. Sprinkle ⅓ of the sugar-flour mixture into the pie shell. Arrange 2 cups sliced fresh or frozen (thawed) peaches on top, then sprinkle with the remaining sugar-flour mixture. Pour 1 cup heavy cream over the top, moving peaches around with a fork to ensure the cream completely covers the mix.

Bake for 45 minutes or until set. Serve warm or chilled.

Pineapple Upsidedown Cake

Recipe notes from Len Berg's cooks called for this dessert to be baked in a 12-inch iron skillet. My mother also made pineapple upside-down cake in an iron skillet, but the restaurant began preparing the popular dessert in a sheet-cake pan to meet the demands of a large commercial operation. This was sometimes printed on the menu as: "Pineapple ǝpᴉsd∩ Cake"

DIRECTIONS

Prepare cake mix as directed on the package. Melt ¼ cup butter in a 9- or 12-inch iron skillet. Sprinkle 1 cup brown sugar to cover the bottom. Arrange pineapple slices in a single layer on top of the sugar and fill in spots with drained, crushed pineapple. Pour cake batter over the top.

Bake at 350 degrees for 40 to 45 minutes or until brown.

Remove from oven and cool. Invert cake onto serving plate and slice.

PINEAPPLE UPSIDEDOWN CAKE

INGREDIENTS

1 box Pillsbury yellow cake mix

eggs, vegetable oil, and water

~~~~

¼ C. butter

1 C. brown sugar

15 oz. can sliced pineapple

8 oz. can crushed pineapple

Strawberry Shortcake

STRAWBERRY SHORTCAKE

INGREDIENTS

1 box Pillsbury yellow cake mix

eggs, vegetable oil, and water

~~~~

1 qt. strawberries, sliced

¼ C. granulated sugar

~~~~

1 C. whipping cream

¼ C. sugar

No matter how often I told myself to skip dessert, when I spotted the waiter or waitress carrying strawberry shortcake to a customer, my resolve failed. This was a popular dessert, but it was one for which I had difficulty finding a "recipe." Jerry Amerson remembered it was the usual Pillsbury yellow cake mix that Len Berg's used for various other desserts; sugar was added to fresh or frozen strawberries; and the special ingredient was the topping of delicious whipped cream.

DIRECTIONS

Prepare cake mix and bake as directed on the package. Remove from sheet cake pan and let cool completely.

Combine 1 quart sliced strawberries (fresh or frozen) with ¼ cup sugar; stir gently and chill.

Beat whipping cream until foamy, gradually adding sugar until soft peaks form.

Cut a serving-size piece of cake, then split it horizontally. Spoon berries and juice over the bottom half and replace the top part of the cake. Spoon more berries and juice on top and finish off with a generous dollop of whipped cream.

Stewed Tomatoes and Okra

Whether they were served alone or paired with rice or okra, stewed tomatoes were a staple of Len Berg's daily selection of vegetables.

DIRECTIONS

Combine 2 ½ cups diced tomatoes, 1 tablespoon sugar, 1 teaspoon salt, dash of pepper, and ¼ cup chopped onions; cook over medium heat for 15 minutes. Strain out 1 cup of juice.

Simmer 1 tablespoon flour and 1 tablespoon butter in skillet or saucepan for about 5 minutes, stirring constantly to prevent browning. Add the cup of reserved juice and simmer until thick. Pour back over the tomatoes.

~~~~~

Wash 1 pound of okra, cut off stems, and slice into ½-inch pieces. Add to the cooked tomatoes and simmer for another 15 to 30 minutes or until okra is tender.

STEWED TOMATOES & OKRA

INGREDIENTS

Stewed tomatoes:

#2 can (2 ½ C.) diced tomatoes

1 Tbsp. sugar

1 tsp. salt

dash pepper

¼ C. chopped onions

~~~~

1 Tbsp. flour

1 Tbsp. butter

~~~~~

1 lb. okra, sliced into ½-inch pieces

Counter seating at Len Berg's. (1983)

A Second Helping

CHAPTER SEVEN

A Place in Memory

Len Berg's Restaurant operated for almost 100 years. When Berg was a young man starting out in 1908, the restaurant where he worked often carried other names, but customers quickly came to refer to each establishment as "Len Berg's place." He operated his business on Macon's Wall Street, yet few people remember anyplace other than the little brick building in an alley behind the Federal Courthouse. By then, Leonard Berg was no longer part of the business, but through the decades, whether operated by Berg, Art Barry, Jeff Amerson, or his son, Jerry, people often returned to Len Berg's Restaurant. When the iconic Southern restaurant closed in 2007, good memories would have to suffice whenever patrons wanted to satisfy their hunger for the good food and friends they had found at Len Berg's.

Years after Len Berg's closing, I can see it in my mind's eye, see the route that takes me there. Whether I am downtown or traveling into Macon on I-75 or I-16, I can take the turns from Broadway or Second Street onto Walnut and see the sign by the alley, the white arrow with green lettering that points to my destination. The striped awning still flutters in the breeze, and in memory, the neon sign promising "Good Food" still sits atop the building. If I am already downtown, I can simply retrace my steps from the Federal Building or the Macon Telegraph,

from the bank or law firm where I find myself on this journey down memory lane.

Before I push open the heavy door, I am greeted by the aroma of onion rings. I squint from the sun reflecting off bumpers of cars lining both sides of the parking lot and prepare to go into the low brick building. Someone holds the door to let a young couple leave, but before he steps out, the man stops to push a button by the door. I enter the crowded restaurant to the sounds of people talking and dishes clattering. I should have expected a crowd since it's already past noon. But at least it's not mid-March and there's not a tour bus full of Cherry Blossom Festival folks ahead of me!

Ah, there's the owner to greet me. He usually speaks to me at some point during every visit even if he isn't the one to show me to my seat. He and his host do a great job of tracking who to seat next, especially since they don't write it down in a log book or anything.

I watch a young family waiting on the bench out front and listen as the mother names the color of each pane of glass. The little girl in her pink dress pats every pane she can reach from where she stands on the low red bench. I stroll down the hall and check the menu propped on the pay phone. It's Monday, so the card is blue. If it was Tuesday or any other day, the menu would be yellow or green or white. The selection changes each day, but always, each item is identified by a letter. I can't count the number of times I've heard folks joke about being so hungry they could eat the entire alphabet or ask why the vegetable soup isn't called alphabet soup. I remember how Jeff Amerson used to put L on the menu at Christmas even though he didn't have any Tomatoes & Okra or Beets in Orange Sauce prepared. When a customer placed their order for C and Y and L, the

waitress cheerily said, "No 'el'! It's Christmas and we have noel, noel, noel."

I return to the front to re-read the article about Chef Wilbur Mitcham and to wait my turn to dine. The host seats a newly arrived party of two ahead of another couple who stand hand in hand next to the family on the bench. The pair explain they are waiting for a particular booth with Connie in Room 2. It's where they were sitting on the day he proposed and she said "Yes" twelve years before.

When I bring friends or family to Len Berg's, I like to sit in a booth in Room 5 or at a table in Room 1 or 4. Since I'm alone and in a hurry today, my favorite spot at the counter will do. As the businessman who had been sitting there leaves, I climb onto the tall stool with its low backrest and hang my purse on the hook beneath the seat. I prop my feet on the low footing and reach for the glass of sweet iced tea Jean has already placed in front of me. She knew that's what I wanted (and that I didn't want any lemon).

Studying the menu, I try to decide: do I want C or H or A? I already know one of the side dishes; Jean probably knows, too. When I'm eating a meat-and-three kind of lunch, I always order the fried corn. In the summer, I sometimes order a cold plate—the fruit bowl with turkey sandwich really hits the spot. This visit, though, I will probably order dessert, especially after seeing Brenda and Tommy take a piece of macaroon pie and strawberry short cake to their customers. Yumm! I decide on the turkey and dressing, turnip greens, and corn.

Jean whisks away with my ticket so the kitchen can prepare my order. She barely missed bumping into Pip, the busboy bringing a rack of clean glasses out of the kitchen, but neither of them seemed to notice the near-collision.

I sip my tea and eavesdrop on the conversation next to me. A couple admires the giant frying pan, the corn-stick pans, ice tongs, and other paraphernalia on the wall behind the counter. The stranger nudges his dining partner and points out the sign suggesting "Kissin' don't last but cookin' do." They talk about the large coffee grinder on the shelf, and I allow myself into their conversation. I tell them about the Idaho potato in a little black pot. "It's really a rock one of the cooks once found in a bag of potatoes."

My visit with strangers is interrupted when Kerry opens the warming drawer on the other side of the counter. A warm yeasty smell aims right for me, and Jean quickly follows suit, putting a roll, a corn stick, and a package of butter on the small plate she sets in front of me. I know it won't be long before I hear someone in the kitchen shout, "Order up, Jean," but I'm so hungry I don't resist the urge to tear into the bread right away.

I am fascinated by the dance taking place behind the counter, like when Jean and Pip almost collided earlier. Miss Mae rings up tickets at the cash register, hands Tommy two quarters, moves a sack of food off the drink box, and makes change for Kerry—all at once! Tommy, who already has two glasses filled with ice in one large hand, inserts the change into a slot in the drink box, pulls out two small glass bottles of Coca-Cola, and pops the top off before lumbering off to deliver drinks to his party in Room 1. I cringe when a new busboy scurrying by with something for the kitchen almost doesn't zig or zag as Brenda pushes open the kitchen carrying three plates of hot food. At least the waitress knows the right steps. So does Miss Ruby, who was reaching into a low cooler under the counter to retrieve something. She avoided the young man as she placed a lemon wedge on the edge of a small white bowl holding a glass of tea.

I can only glimpse through narrow windows into the kitchen, but I wonder what the dance must be like in there? As Willie pushes the *door open to bring out fresh tea for the dispenser, I see how narrow and crowded that space is and consider the number of plates they must prepare each day. It must be hot in there, too. There are cooks and a dishwasher, the busboys and wait staff, all moving past a fry pot full of hot grease, a stove top and steam table filled with pots, and ovens where Annette is baking more bread.*

I come to attention when Jean pushes back through the kitchen doors and sets a plate in front of me. Mmm. Turkey and dressing with cranberry sauce, and it's not even Thanksgiving! I can enjoy a favorite holiday treat year-round. It's filling, and I almost resist dessert. As I dab the corners of my mouth with the soft white napkin, I see Brenda put a plate of hot fudge cake with a candle on a small turntable. It's someone's birthday! Okay, now I must have dessert. Do I want chocolate pie, cherry cobbler, or macaroon pie?

Now that I'm stuffed, I drain the last of my tea and wave Jean off so she doesn't fill it again. I lay the napkin on the counter and turn to see people waiting for a seat in the still-crowded restaurant. It's a little after 1:30, and the restaurant doesn't close for another hour. I see one of the hosts jot a note on a scrap of paper as a new party enters the building. Before he puts it in his shirt pocket, I catch a glimpse. He wrote: "pink tie: 4" below "two suits" and the crossed through "little girl: 3" that must have noted the party who arrived before me.

I turn around to say goodbye to Jean, who waves and places a fresh napkin and place setting in front of the new customer who took the seat I just left. I make my way to the door and a stranger pulls it open for me. As I start to walk through, I can't resist. The small sign with black lettering beckons, and though I wonder if the busy kitchen even hears the sound, I am obliged to "Press Button to Praise Cook."

Friends, family, employees, and customers will long remember their own journeys to Len Berg's, recalling the people and atmosphere of the place. Some will smile when the man with a familiar face confirms, "Yes, I used to be with Len Berg's Restaurant," or when they reminisce with family about celebrations they shared in Macon. A local business person, being interviewed, will respond to a question about the best meal she ever had in central Georgia as "…at Len Berg's downtown when I worked at Charter Medical." Internet sites monitored in faraway places continue to list the restaurant as a favorite destination in Macon, even though it has been closed now for several years. Certainly, people will remember the restaurant, the special people and special times. And they remember the food.

Former Len Berg's patrons will start New Year's Day with a dish of black-eyed peas for luck or recall the pink whipped cream topping their macaroon pie during the Cherry Blossom Festival. Holding a fuzzy fresh Georgia peach will remind some people of H.M.F.P.I.C. and the official start to a Macon summer. Autumn may bring memories of a UGA tailgate party with a fried chicken cold plate that included a pimiento cheese sandwich and deviled egg. Turkey and dressing during Thanksgiving and Christmas will remind them of Len Berg's, and year-round, they might think of the lemon or chocolate meringue pie, the filet mignon, stuffed shrimp, carrot and raisin salad, macaroni and cheese and more.

As they hold Len Berg's as a place in memory, many people will think of the building, the people, the celebrations, and more, but they will hold closest their memories of Len Berg's food.

Peach Ice Cream

PEACH ICE CREAM

INGREDIENTS

1 Qt. fresh peaches, puréed

3 C. sugar

7 C. half-and-half

3 Tbsp. lemon juice

¼ tsp. salt

1 tsp. almond flavoring

In the late 1970s, Jeff Amerson purchased a billboard to appear the first day of June. All it said was, "H.M.F.P.I.C. You Know Where." This, along with a small ad in the newspaper, served as a reminder to the community of a special treat.

Len Berg's Restaurant served Home-Made Fresh Peach Ice Cream—the mysterious H.M.F.P.I.C.—during summer months when the restaurant could procure the best peaches from local orchards. The tradition began around 1960 when a visitor from out of state asked for peach ice cream. Since they didn't have it on the menu, Art Barry and Jeff Amerson called around to find a packing plant with fresh peaches for the customer. The owner of Bateman's Peach Packing House encouraged the restaurateurs to add peach ice cream to their menu, and Chef Mitcham tested a recipe from Duncan Hines' Adventures in Good Cooking. Each year, Len Berg's staff made a test batch from fresh local peaches and offered a taste-test to customers on May 31, the day before the ice cream officially appeared on the menu. Then, for the next six to eight weeks, customers could order a "little bit" or a "big bit" of H.M.F.P.I.C. to enjoy at the end of their meal. Many were sorry to see peach season end in July.

One year, Georgia suffered devastating losses to the peach crop. Jerry Amerson altered the trademark ad to say: "H.M.?.P.I.C. You Know Where." When asked about the question mark, Amerson explained he wasn't certain if they would use fresh, frozen, or foreign (non-Georgia) peaches, but he knew it was June and Len Berg's customers expected their Peach Ice Cream.

DIRECTIONS

Using the freshest, sweetest peaches available, peel, slice, and purée 1 quart of the fruit. Add 3 cups of sugar, 7 cups of half-and-half, 3 tablespoons lemon juice, ¼ teaspoon salt, and 1 teaspoon of almond flavoring. Allow the mixture to sit in the refrigerator several hours or overnight before putting into the mixer of an ice cream churn.

Follow directions for churning the ice cream to a wonderful frozen treat.

Chef Wilbur Mitcham dipping up H.M.F.P.I.C.

A Second Helping

Author's Note

Growing up, my brother John used to tease that when—or if—I ever married, my poor husband might go hungry. He figured the only thing I could do in the kitchen was bake brownies. When I joined the Len Berg's Restaurant extended family in 1979, my brother was relieved.

So was my mother, who learned not to ask what I was cooking. Instead, each afternoon when we talked, she wanted to know what Jerry brought home for supper. My entire family looked forward to our contribution to holiday dinners, the turkey and dressing, the apple and macaroon pies. Even the vendor who embroidered shirts for Len Berg's recognized my only role in the restaurant business; he created a special hat for me. It said, "Len Berg's Official Taster."

So, dear reader, my restaurant experience is based on my perspective as an observer. But during the many years as a taster (and the spouse of a restaurateur), I learned a lot about what it takes to keep a restaurant going.

I have tremendous respect for the men and women who keep a busy kitchen clean and functioning well, alongside the talented cooks who prepare the food. I marvel at waiters and waitresses who serve multiple parties at once, managing to keep varied orders straight and a smile on their face. I admire managers who juggle schedules, budgets, and a multitude of details, yet appear as if they have the best job in the world. My appreciation goes out also, of course, to the customers who make their favorite diner a success and help keep independent restaurateurs in business.

After being associated with an iconic Southern restaurant for twenty-four years, you might think I could make great salmon croquettes or a delicious filet mignon. But I think I'll leave that to the real restaurateurs. I'm just happy to share a few recipes and stories to help you remember Len Berg's Restaurant.

Oh, but I can bake a really good brownie.

Marie's Brownie Recipe

MARIE'S BROWNIES

INGREDIENTS

1 C. shortening

2 C. sugar

4 eggs

1 tsp. vanilla

4 to 5 Tbsp. cocoa

1 ½ C. self-rising flour

1 C. chopped pecans

I learned to bake brownies when I joined a local 4-H Club in rural Georgia. Perhaps practice does help us perfect our baking endeavors. My father-in-law especially enjoyed this brownie warm and served with a scoop of vanilla ice cream.

DIRECTIONS

Preheat oven to 350 degrees.

In a large bowl, mix 1 cup shortening and 2 cups sugar until blended; add 4 beaten eggs, one at a time. Stir in 1 teaspoon vanilla and 4 to 5 tablespoons cocoa. Add 1 ½ cups self-rising flour and mix well. Add 1 cup chopped pecans.

Pour mixture into a well-greased 9- x 13-inch baking dish. Bake for about 35 to 45 minutes, or until a toothpick comes out almost clean. (A little moisture on the toothpick results in a moister brownie, and after practicing, you'll find the right amount of doneness to suit your tastes.)

Cool for at least 10 minutes before you cut and remove from the pan.

Enjoy—and may you always remember Len Berg's Restaurant!

Resources

Personal Interviews

Celia Amerson to Marie Amerson, September 2009 to May 2011. Personal interviews in author's possession.

Jerry Amerson to Marie Amerson, September 2009 to May 2011 and June 2019. Personal interviews in author's possession.

Arthur P. Barry Jr. to Marie Amerson, December 2009. Personal interview in author's possession.

Leonard Lee Berg to Marie Amerson, September 2009 and May 2011. Personal interviews by telephone and e-mail correspondence; in author's possession.

Susan Berg Frizell to Marie Amerson. September 2009 and May 2011. Personal interviews by telephone and e-mail correspondence; in author's possession.

Mary Anne Berg Richardson to Marie Amerson. September 2009 and May 2011. Personal interviews by telephone and e-mail correspondence; in author's possession.

Other Sources

Alva, Marilyn. "Len Berg's: Specializing in 'down-home' cooking," *Nation's Restaurant News.* (7 October 1985).

Anderson, George David. *A City Comes of Age: An Urban Study of Macon, Georgia, During the 1920s.* 1975.

Anderson, Nancy B. *Macon Pictorial History.* 1979.

Bragg, Rick. *The Best Cook in the World … Tales from My Momma's Table.* (Alfred A. Knopf, 2018).

Cutler, Bill. "For Home Cooking, Macon's the Place," *Georgia Trend.* (May 1986).

Hines, Duncan and Clara W. Hines. *Adventures in Good Cooking and the Art of Carving in the Home.* 1957.

Howard, Maria Willett. *Lowney's Cookbook.* 1908.

"Len Berg's Does Southern Food Right," *Southern Living.* (January 1997).

Lewis, Arthur. Unpublished typed article signed by "Historian" and cited in article about the construction of the new Len Berg's building. Dated 1950.

Macon Telegraph. 1907-2007. Archives.

Mariani, John. *America Eats Out: An Illustrated History of Restaurants, Taverns, Coffee Shops, Speakeasies, and Other Establishments That Have Fed Us for 350 Years*. 1991.

Mayes, Frances. *Under the Tuscan Sun* (Random House, 1996).

New Georgia Encyclopedia. www.georgiaencyclopedia.org.

Polk's Macon City Directory (1899-1969). Polk, R.L. & Company Publishers.

Reagan, Frank et al. *History of Macon. The First One Hundred Years 1823-1923*. reprinted in 2007 by Peyton Anderson Foundation.

"Sanborn Fire Insurance Map of Downtown Macon: 1923 Corrected to 1939."

Sanborn Fire Insurance Maps for Georgia Towns and Cities, 1884-1922: Macon, Georgia." 1908, Sheet 8.

"Romancing in Business," addressed to "% News, Macon, Georgia." Unpublished article (author unknown) from personal collection of Berg family. 1934.

US Census 1910 and 1920, prepared by, Bureau of the Census, Washington DC.

Vaccaro, Pamela J. *Beyond the Ice Cream Cone: The Whole Scoop on Food at the 1904 World's Fair* (Enid Press, 2004).

Wenzel, George L. Sr. *Wenzel's Menu Maker*, 2nd ed. (1979).

Young, Ida, Julius Gholson, and Clara Nell Hargrove. *History of Macon, Georgia (1823-1949) (1950)*.

INDEX OF RECIPES

INDEX

Matchbook from Len Berg's noting that
"Particular People dine at Len Berg's in
the Post Office Alley,
Macon, Georgia." (1955)

Made in the USA
Monee, IL
09 August 2021